FINDING PEACE IN AN OUT OF CONTROL WORLD

A HOW TO BOOK ON BEING AT PEACE REGARDLESS OF WHAT LIFE THROWS YOUR WAY

By
Cindy Nolte

DEDICATION

In memory of my dear friend who left this planet far too soon. Thank you for always loving me unconditionally and for teaching me to look on the bright side of every obstacle that I encounter. I will always love you for being one of my truest friends. I hope that this book brings as much joy to others as your wonderful light brought to all those who knew you.

And

In memory of my maternal grandparents, who were two of the most generous people I have ever known. You both did too much for me to ever list. I am forever grateful for having had you in my life.

ACKNOWLEDGMENTS

I would like to thank my teachers and mentors along the way who have inspired me to "be better" so I can be of better service to those I am meant to reach.

I would like to thank my husband (Jerry), my mom, my dad, and my brothers for their love and support. You did not always understand the way I think, but you have always loved me just the way I am. Together, you create a safety net that reminds me I am loved. Some people wait their whole lives to feel the way I do because of you. Without any of you, I may not have had the courage to ignore the many critics along the way.

I would also like to recognize my wonderful friends who have encouraged me even when my ideas may not have been the norm. You all hold a place in my heart.

To each and every individual mentioned, my heart overflows with love and gratitude to you. You all have taken part in making me the person I am today. I am blessed!

—Cindy C. Nolte

Table of Contents

A NOTE TO MY READERS

If you picked up this book and asked, "What makes this different, even better, than other self-help books?" I would reply that, "I'm not coming from a telling stance or even claiming that your life will be perfect if you read this book. I live what I teach, and I have learned to navigate through whatever life throws at me and keep my peace. I have learned through trial and error how to live my life rather than just existing." Through the lessons that I have outlined on these pages, that is what I invite you to experience, too. So in other words, if you are looking for a no-nonsense, realistic approach to living your ordinary life in extraordinary ways, even with obstacles along the way, that is what I have learned to do and what I share with you in this book.

When I decided to make helping others my livelihood, I made a choice never to give advice I wouldn't take myself. This was one of the toughest things I have ever had to do, but the benefits have turned out to be limitless. I found that this credo forced me to grow and see life in a new way. It's easier for people to *give* advice than to take it themselves. I believe in teaching others strong lessons by demonstrating *why* those lessons I teach are worth learning. If *I* don't think the lesson is important enough to use it in my own life, why would a student be excited about learning it from *me*? That's why the tips in this book come from the lessons I've learned on my spiritual journey—ones I use every day in my own life. My life is a testament to the concepts that I teach. Although you will all have unique experiences on your journeys, I have found there is a formula that can be applied to anything that comes your way.

The ideas in this book can help you take back your power, connect with yourself, feel strong connections within, and recognize that everything has a purpose. Coming from that perspective, you will not only believe that everything will be okay, you'll also *feel* it and *live* it every day. You will gain tools to use in your life to assist you in navigating through obstacles and gaining clarity regarding what is "right" for you. You will learn how to be at peace in your life regardless of what challenges you face. You will learn that it is not about having the perfect life, but acknowledging that each experience fits in to your life in a perfect way to create the life you are meant to have in that moment. The step-by-step instructions in this book will walk you through how to acknowledge these ideas and, know in your heart how they relate to you.

By writing this book, I don't pretend to have all the answers. You don't need all the answers at this moment. *Nobody* needs to have all the answers to all the questions all the time. Rather, I share an equation for being at peace even if you don't know everything, a way to find your inner awareness and gain access to answers that already lie within you. Once you tap in to your own inner-knowing, your life will flow. You'll recognize how the pieces of your life fall into place. Events in your life will mirror what your inner guidance is whispering to you. You'll find peace in knowing that every part of your life serves a purpose. You'll find security in feeling it and experiencing it.

That doesn't mean you'll never experience disappointment. But when you experience true inner-knowing, you will realize that even unpleasant experiences serve a purpose in your life's bigger picture. That brings comfort.

Finding this inner-knowing can be a lot less complicated than it sounds. If you follow what this book places before you, your discovery process can be an enjoyable experience. I urge you to remember that life is a classroom. We are all here to learn. You will receive lessons throughout your whole life. Although the lessons are unending, when we are present we can enjoy each moment for what it is meant to be. Slow down and take pleasure in the process. Life is a marathon; it is not a sprint.

Enjoy your journey!

—Cindy

INTRODUCTION

The world can seem out of control if we get caught up in all that's going on. It's easy to get pulled into the media frenzy about crime, the global economy, international relations, and the fast pace of today's society. Even if we're able to block out these influences, our inner world can seem tumultuous with all the demands placed on us. The chaos can leave us uneasy, stressed, and in search of peace. Through years of study and working with clients, I have found the solution to peace lies *within*. Knowing what lies within requires connecting with your true self. For many, that is far easier said than done.

Why is it difficult? An overwhelming number of people allow others to make the bulk of the major decisions in their lives. They don't trust their own judgment to know what's best for them. Another large percentage of people think making decisions only based on their immediate happiness is all that matters. Some people lack self-esteem, question themselves, or lose touch with what they want. Others have even forgotten what good ol' moral values are. All of these actions create inner turmoil and separate individuals from their true selves.

The goal is to uncover the true beauty that lies within you and knows the secrets to your own happiness, prosperity, and peace. When you reconnect with this beauty—your soul, your inner- knowing, your true self, your connection to your Creator—it doesn't matter what else is going on. You can stay in your natural state of joy and peace. This process removes all of the negative feelings--like guilt, fear, or anxiety--that go along with making a decision, because when you are truly acting in accordance with what is best for your soul, it never harms anyone else. Connecting with your soul is harder than it sounds. Through years of conditioning, you have been taken further and further away from who you truly are. This book takes you through a fun-filled discovery process that will leave you reunited with your true self, teach you what it is to live with passion, restore the "flow" in your life, and ultimately bring you peace.

Notice of layoff

1~Finding Yourself Through the Clutter

Self-reflection often occurs around birthdays, the end of the year, or noteworthy events in our lives. Individuals frequently struggle through the process with the unrest of "should haves" in their lives. Personal reflection can be beneficial, but when reflection causes disruption it can be a sign of other underlying issues—like being uncomfortable in your own skin.

The key to reflection, much like many other things in life, is moderation. Too much reflection can cause you to get stuck in the past, keep you in a holding pattern, and even lead you to punish yourself for what you did or didn't do. If you don't view yourself the same way as you would a loving friend, any period of reflection can cause unrest within your life. Some people are too hard on themselves.

Others may decide to avoid the process altogether and force themselves into self-destructive behaviors that distract them from what is really going on. Looking outside of yourself only creates a bandage for what's really going on inside. True happiness starts from within; that's where peace resides. Many people search outside of themselves to find what's missing. They feel empty, yet never slow down to figure out what that emptiness means.

Perhaps they've been taught to need instant gratification. When something feels awry, they often add more to the equation.

We constantly hear about celebrities—and even people we know—having affairs in an effort to fill the void they feel. Some use food, alcohol, and other substances in excess. Others resist downtime so they don't have to face how empty their lives feel to them.

Over the course of our lives, we create depths of illusion through all of this excess that distracts us from our own truth. In most cases, adding doesn't fix anything. Do these individuals even recognize who they see in the mirror, let alone love the person they see looking back? Do they know what they enjoy? Do they know what their passions are? People are out in the world making significant financial decisions, leading organizations, saving lives, and so on, but many have lost sight of who they truly are or even why they are doing what they do. Others are making everything and everyone else in their life more important than they are. Some are taught that self-sacrifice is the only way to get ahead or that thinking of themselves is selfish. For others, putting a magnifying glass on who they truly are can be scary.

The reality is that it is exhausting to pretend. It takes work to be somebody other than who you are. It takes more energy to act like somebody other than who you are, and the added *fluff* just creates more confusion, further draining an already-depleted self. It becomes tiring just to get up in the morning. That is because you are expending energy on forcing yourself to be somebody you aren't, and you are trying to meet your life's demands with whatever energy is left.

We can't blame these individuals for getting into this situation; they've had help. Take, for example, slogging through a growing forty-plus-hour work-week and enduring the pressure to stand out among your colleagues or climb the proverbial ladder, just for starters. Adding to the clutter, many people have children to raise, extracurricular activities to support, other family demands to meet, and rising inflation rates to battle. Plus they have to deal with the *advice* of friends and family on how to handle it all. Do you get the idea?

I'm convinced that many people know they aren't living authentically. Consider the current self-help craze. The next time you're at someone's home, chances are you will find several self-help books on their bookshelves. There are local book clubs sharing ideas on these books, workshops, lectures, DVDs, and CDs. Individuals are seeking change, and they want to know how to achieve it. Some people become so daunted by the *perceived* work needed to get back in touch with themselves that they never get beyond purchasing the book itself. Let's face it; they know it's too tiring to work hard at anything else in their lives. You need real answers that can be applied to real lives, not advice from somebody who can take hours out of their day or months out of their year to go on a spiritual pilgrimage.

Yet getting in touch with oneself doesn't have to be hard work. The journey can be an amazing discovery process if you allow it to be. When you begin to uncover who you are without judgment, you will see the beauty that lies within. Each of us is beautiful on the inside when stripped of the pretense of armor that the outside world has covered us with. There is great comfort in knowing who you are and truly liking yourself. There is an ease that is brought out when you allow yourself to be who you are without paying attention to who others expect you to be.

When going through this process, it will be important for you to fit some quiet time into your schedule. This will allow you to connect with who you are without fear or pressure from outside forces. During this downtime, you will find that simplifying—the simple act of just "being"—will bring clarity to you. In this fast-paced world, it is important to give yourself permission to wind down even for just a few moments; nobody can be "on" all of the time. The more you schedule it, this quiet time will come to be something you crave. You get to focus on yourself for a change.

To get in touch with the inner "you," go through the exercises in each chapter of this book. The chapters offer guidelines and activities to help you get where you want to go in your own way. The examples of the exercises were provided by clients who agreed to share their information. Completing the exercises will help you uncover the things that you are passionate about. Then, after you have finished reading the book, you can spend the downtime that you have come to crave doing those things. It's a process, just like climbing the proverbial ladder or building a life with family and friends. The closer you get to yourself and the more layers you strip away, the quicker the process will happen. It's amazing how fast you can travel without those "should haves" weighing you down.

While you embark on this journey, I encourage you to enjoy the process and appreciate what you discover without pressuring yourself to be *done*. Enjoy each step; that is what life is about.

2~Tuning in to Your Spirit
Through Meditative Practices

I don't claim to be a yogi or to have studied with all of the great masters of meditation, but I do believe that meditation is something your body knows how to do automatically—like breathing or pumping blood through your veins. My perspective is that we are not learning, but rather remembering, how to meditate. This is our birthright; it is a powerful tool in connecting with ourselves and our Creator.

Also, I've never been a *rule* person and probably never will be. So if you've studied or attempted meditation and thought it was *too complicated* or you just weren't *getting it,* I invite you to throw out all of the rules. My motto for learning most things is this:

If it works for you, use it. If it doesn't work for you, throw it out.

Chances are, if you grew up in North America, you weren't practicing formal meditation as a child. I would argue, however, that you did involuntarily practice *informal meditation*. Formal meditation is the practice of consciously emptying one's mind, while informal meditation is a calming of one's mind through activities that we partake in within our everyday lives.

These informal activities might include walking, running, gardening, horseback riding, or other activities that allow you to go inward and quiet your mind. Think of the times you daydreamed and let your mind drift off into another world without trying. Recall an occasion that you jogged in nature after a long day at work, and before you knew it, you felt like you were floating along your running path without a care in the world. The act of being alone doing something you love allows you to escape the negative impact of almost anything you may have experienced earlier in the day, taking you into the present time; now there is just you and your run. In effect, your spirit cares for you in a way that is quite natural. It takes you inward to escape anything unpleasant and brings you forward on a journey to the now-present tense.

I suggest that we meditate *informally* more than we may realize. Informal meditation starts with being comfortable with silence and is a way to prep your body-mind-spirit for formal meditation. Experiment! Ride in your car without the radio on or without having a conversation on your cell phone. I am not advising you to practice formal meditation while driving; you know you need to pay attention to the road. Just get used to fewer distractions in your life.

Rediscover yourself while rediscovering what has always been around you. Nature is great for connecting with spirit. Movement can be helpful when you become stuck in your thoughts; just take a walk outside or ride your bike. Find *something* you enjoy doing and do it in silence. I get so much great insight while just enjoying a run or walk in nature. The activity you select isn't important. But as you're doing whatever you choose, pay attention to the thoughts that come to you. Often you will get new solutions to old problems. As you retrain your mind to tune into this tool, you will find that insight may begin to flow more and more easily as you wind down. Eventually this insight will flow automatically as your body-mind-spirit begins to remember how to work in harmony. This awareness was always there for your asking. You just were unable to hear it in the past, perhaps.

When you're ready to take the reins, move on to formal meditation. Create a ritual around what you've already been doing. When you first start, make sure you choose the same room or outside location, and choose the same time of day. Then once your meditation becomes habitual, it won't matter where you are or what time it is. It's like developing tone in your muscles; you want to get your body, mind, and spirit acclimated to this new practice through consistency of place and time.

When you are prepared, ask your body-mind-spirit to guide you through the process. First, you will want to focus on relaxing your body and then on quieting your mind. If you feel it is difficult to connect to spirit, go back to who you were as a child before you were conditioned to move away from your spirit. Remember the "you" who so easily could daydream and bring yourself anywhere that your mind could imagine. Some individuals have found it helpful to imagine their souls connecting to their daydreaming childhood selves and then asking that version of themselves to escort them on their meditation. Just allow yourself to begin to relax however it makes sense to you.

Concentrate on your breathing. Notice how your breath gently slows down. Have faith that your body-mind-spirit knows what it needs to do to guide you through this process. If irrelevant thoughts, often referred to as "monkey thoughts," come into your mind, say, "Thank You," and let them go. Watch them float away like leaves down a stream or balloons into the sky. If an issue arises that you are guided to address, I invite you to meditate on it. Notice that in this state of stillness, a new perspective to old obstacles can arise. Once you allow this insight to flow, let that go too for the time being. Allow yourself to just be free of whatever happened in the past or might happen in the future; just be in the present.

It may be necessary for you to take baby steps to prepare your mind to take part in formal meditation. Guided meditations can sometimes be a nice stepping stone for individuals who desire some assistance in getting to a meditative state. Once you find that place of stillness, some consider it easier to get there in the future.

Often people ask me why they can't quiet their minds completely. I say, "Maybe it's not time." Think about having a conversation with an old friend to whom you haven't spoken in months or even years. Regard meditation as a nonstop conversation going from one topic to another in an effort to catch up. If you've just decided you'd like to sit down and meditate for the first time in your life, I would guess your spirit has something to say to its long-lost friend. Listen to it! You'll be amazed at what comes to you. Your mind will become quieter over time and, as obstacles arise, you'll have this amazing tool at your disposal.

I believe that the best advice often lies within; sometimes we just need help uncovering it. We know what's truly best for us when we are connected with spirit. These are the nuggets we discover that we just know to be true. Meditation can assist us in experiencing this connection.

Indeed, meditation completely changed my outlook on life, allowing me to create balance in my life and gain perspective on what occurs around me. I am human. I still get angry, hurt, or upset at times, but when I do, I realize that putting out negativity doesn't serve me, and I'm usually able to bounce back to a state of peace rather quickly. I can handle crisis situations better than before I started meditating. And during meditation, the *good stuff* is magnified.

As people begin to meditate, they often get a glow about them—the kind you see when somebody lights up a room with that certain *something*. That lovely glow reflects their soul, and it's just as beautiful in every one of us. Before long, you'll discover that meditation helps bring about a change in people's confidence, the way they carry themselves, their outlook on life, and the sparkle in their eyes.

While individuals meditate, I remind them to be aware of the energy in the room and around them. Anyone who has walked into a room after a disagreement and felt the tension knows that emotions have energy. This energy leaves a wake where you've been and can affect others. You have experienced this if your mood has ever changed for no apparent reason and you find it matches that of another person you recently encountered. It can be an uplifting feeling you get from a positive group meeting; it can be the moodiness you may feel shopping in a crowded mall during the holidays. Examples are endless.

As a result of this energy, I incorporate the *Always Use Protection* rule into my meditative practices. I always get giggles from my students when I talk about this rule. Energy protection during meditation can be likened to practicing safe sex. If we forget to protect ourselves in either case, we can leave ourselves open to negative energy entering our lives. So call it what you will, just remember to practice "safe meditation."

Whenever you're opening yourself up to the world around you, you are open to both the negative and the positive. The world is made up of dualities, and energy is no different. It is not created because you are on a spiritual journey. You just become more aware of it as a result and now can take steps to keep your energy at a high vibration (positive).

The steps to protecting yourself are quite easy and, once practiced, can help you avoid picking up on others' emotions—not only in your home during your meditative practices but anywhere you go. I use them daily! This protection will act as a barrier to prevent only negativity. It will not impede the flow of positive emotions like love and joy in any way.

Here are a few ways to *Always Use Protection*:

- Call on your guides. If you believe in angels, Archangel Michael or St. Michael is the one you would call on for protection.

- Picture the white light of whoever you believe is your Creator and surround yourself from the top of your head down through your body, filling your heart and then filling your whole body to the tips of your toes with that light. Allow this light to fill every cell of your body and beam from every pore up to four feet all around your entire body as if you are placing yourself in a protective cocoon of your Creator's light.

- If you can't envision it, feel it, or sense it, just know that it is there as long as you ask for it.

- Close your eyes as you do this and picture or sense yourself fully encompassed in the white light. Envision the white light around your body at a full arm's length out on all sides to protect your aura and etheric fields.

- Allow your breath to slow down and your body to relax.

- Be confident that protection is available through your Creator, whoever you believe that to be. All you have to do is ask for it.

- If you are having a hard time imagining the shield, slow down and allow your body to "see it" in your mind's eye. If you can't see it, feel it like a warm protective blanket all around you.

- If you can't feel it, just "know" it is there for your asking, and imagine where it is as your Creator begins to encompass you in protective light.

- When you slow down and just allow what is there for your asking, it will come.

- Pray if it is in your belief system to do so, and ask God for protection.

- If the previous steps do not resonate with you, use your own visualization to picture yourself fully protected, guarded, and safe.

Once this protective light envelops you like a warm blanket, just allow yourself to enjoy the comfort of it for a moment.

The next step is to give energy to the seven major chakras to strengthen and support this protection. Chakras are the energy centers of your body. The seven major chakras are found up the center of the body along the spine, starting at the root chakra (base of your spine) and ending at the crown chakra (top of your head). Each chakra is represented by a different color. The easiest way to remember the colors of the chakras is the same way you may have been told to remember the colors of the rainbow in school (Roy G. Biv = Red, Orange, Yellow, Green, Blue, Indigo, Violet).

There is a detailed illustration of the chakras, their locations, and their colors on the next page. As shown, the first major chakra (1—root) is located at the base of the spine and is red in color. The second major chakra (2—sacral) is orange in color. The third major chakra (3—solar plexus) is yellow in color. The fourth major chakra (4—heart) is green in color. The fifth major chakra (5—throat) is blue in color. The sixth major chakra is (6—brow or third eye) is indigo in color. The seventh major chakra (7—crown) is violet in color.

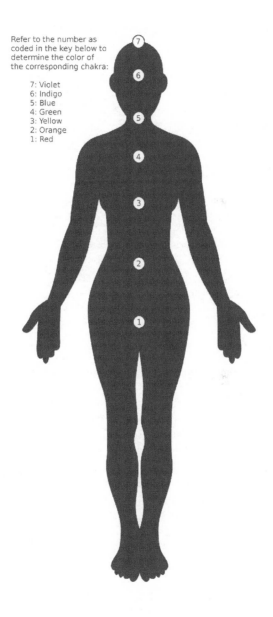

Refer to the number as coded in the key below to determine the color of the corresponding chakra:

7: Violet
6: Indigo
5: Blue
4: Green
3: Yellow
2: Orange
1: Red

When I say "give energy to the chakras," I mean to do that in whatever way resonates most with you. You can do it by calling on the energy of your Creator, asking Him or Her to energize those key areas of your body, or by just focusing on them one at a time and asking for energy to be restored to them. It may be uplifting or calming when this process takes place. Remember, you will get whatever you need. If your body is in need of energy, that is what you will probably experience. If your body is in need of calmness, you will probably experience a dialing down of energy, so to speak. Just allow your Creator to care for you in the way you have requested. Don't get hung up on the details.

Finally, when you feel fully surrounded in protection and your chakras feel energized, picture a beam of light shining through your crown chakra (the top of your head) all the way down your body through your feet, fastening you firmly to the ground. Imagine yourself so secure that no one could push you over, like a mighty tree that is unaffected by the strongest of winds. Now you're ready to begin your meditation.

Meditation will come naturally when you allow it to. Use these pointers when starting your meditation practice:

- Choose a time that works well for you daily.

- Wear comfortable clothes.

- Turn off phones and other distracting items.

- Keep your eyes open, or close them. Experiment to see which works better for you.

- Decide what type of music you want, choosing music that doesn't have words. That way, you won't be thinking of the words instead of focusing on meditating.

- Sit in a comfortable position. (Ideally, when you meditate it is best to sit with your spine in alignment. If that is not comfortable for you, choose another position rather than deciding not to meditate or allowing your seated position to take away from the experience.) If you don't, you will focus on the discomfort rather than the meditation.

- Make sure you can count on being left alone. Ensure that this time is yours and yours alone.

Start your meditation by concentrating on your breathing, relaxing your body and then clearing your mind. With your eyes open or closed, as you prefer, you can say a mantra over and over like *Om* or *Peace* if you desire—whatever works for you.

You may find it helps you to focus on one single thing: a babbling brook, a flower, or a blank spot on the wall. You may prefer to keep your eyes closed. You will soon determine what feels right to you.

Imagine a ray of light coming down from your Creator through your crown chakra (the top of your head) and through your body, connecting directly to your soul, located in your heart chakra (the center of your chest).

Name the parts of your body from the top of your head to the tips of your toes, guiding each to relax individually until you get to a state of relaxation. Doing this can help you relax your body and then your mind.

Here's an order you might follow:

- Focus on your breathing.

- Relax the top of your head.

- Relax your forehead.

- Relax your eyes.

- Relax your cheeks.

- Unclench your teeth.

- Relax your chin.

- Relax your neck.

- Relax your shoulders.

- Relax your upper arms.

- Relax your elbows.

- Relax your lower arms.

- Relax your wrists.

- Relax your hands all the way down to the tips of your fingers.

- Relax your upper back.

- Relax the middle of your back.

- Relax your lower back.

- Relax your chest.

- Relax your stomach.

- Relax your hips.

- Relax your thighs.

- Relax your knees.

- Relax your calves.

- Relax your ankles.

- Relax your feet all the way to the tips of your toes.

- Relax your whole body.

- BREATHE!

- If there is any area of your body that does not feel completely relaxed, breathe into it and allow it to catch up to the other areas.

- Close your eyes if you would like to.

When you're in the meditative state and connected to your Creator, it's possible you will experience an intense feeling of unconditional love unlike any human love. If you've never felt anything close to this before, it can seem overwhelming—even bringing you to tears. Just know this: as long as it feels comforting and peaceful, you're making the right connection.

Allow your mind to adjust to the slowness of your breath. Allow your mind to relax. Be still in the peace, love, and security of connecting to your Creator. Allow any extraneous thoughts that drift into your mind to sail away; doing this will bring you back to your intended focus of stillness.

When you begin this practice, try meditating for five minutes, and build up from there. If you live a fast-paced life, it may take you more than five minutes to relax. The more you practice, the quicker you will be able to get to a relaxed state, the longer you'll be able to meditate, and the fewer unnecessary thoughts will permeate your mind. Doing meditation well—like the other techniques in this book—takes practice. Know that you will progress on the schedule that is just right for you, and that all is exactly as it is meant to be. Give yourself permission to enjoy the progress you make at each moment. There is no competition in meditation or spiritual development.

When mastered, this practice is one of the most powerful tools you can use at any time to find peace in an out-of-control world. When you are truly in a state of peace, you're able to trust that your life has direction. You're able to see that you're exactly where you're supposed to be.

When you do your best and don't get the desired results, you're able to accept that it wasn't meant to be and that something better is coming. You don't always get the best of everything, but you will get what was meant for you.

You trust in the laws of the universe or your Creator. You ask for guidance and know everything will come together when the time is right. You feel a connection to something outside of yourself even when you're alone. And once you feel that union, you can't help but feel like you are part of something: complete, unconditional love.

It's both peace and comfort—the most amazing feelings you've ever felt all at the same time.

Quick-Reference Steps to Meditation

1) **Protect Yourself**

2) **Relax Your Body**

- Focus on your breathing.

- Relax the top of your head.

- Relax your forehead.

- Relax your eyes.

- Relax your cheeks.

- Make sure that your teeth are not clenched.

- Relax your chin.

- Relax your neck.

- Relax your shoulders.

- Relax your upper arms.

- Relax your elbows.

- Relax your lower arms.

- Relax your wrists.

- Relax your hands all the way down to the tips of your fingers.

- Relax your upper back.

- Relax the middle of your back.

- Relax your lower back.

- Relax your chest.

- Relax your stomach.

- Relax your hips.

- Relax your thighs.

- Relax your knees.

- Relax your calves.

- Relax your ankles.

- Relax your feet all the way to the tips of your toes.

- Relax your whole body.

- BREATHE!

- Close your eyes if you would like to.

3) **Relax Your Mind**

- Stare at an object.

- Stare at a blank spot on the wall.

- Close your eyes and listen to a waterfall.

- Focus inward with eyes closed (I focus on my heart center).

Practice for five minutes, and build as you feel comfortable.

4) **Do you have monkey thoughts? What can you do to release them?**

If it is a relevant thought, consider solutions that come to you.

If it is not important right then, just say, "Thank you," and let them fade away however seems right to you...

You might envision one of these:

- A leaf floating down a brook

- A balloon drifting up into the sky

- Waves erasing a message on a sandy beach

3~Intuition: Connecting
with Your Creator

Now that you have a sense of meditation, where do you go from here? The more *connected* you become to spirit, the more you'll be able to *hear* what your guides, your Creator, or angels are trying to tell you. This is referred to as intuition.

The idea of intuition can raise a variety of emotions, depending on what your understanding or past experiences with it may be. The immediate response for some may be to think of the boardwalk or storefront psychic with a neon sign in his or her front window. My view of intuition is very different. I believe it to be a gentle communication between individuals and their Creator. It is inner guidance brought about by your connection with the Divine, whoever you believe that to be. Although for some it is helpful to get clarification from others, advising individuals is not the primary purpose of such a gift. The main reason for us to have intuitive guidance is for each of us to have the ability to communicate with our Higher Power for direction along our life path.

Everyone is here for a reason, and our Creator is trying to guide us on our path to fulfill that purpose. Intuition acts as our internal dialogue or lifeline with our Creator to assist us along our way. As we allow the connection to strengthen, it can act as our internal GPS through life.

First and foremost, intuition is not a gift for only a chosen few. Everyone has this gift. It just lies dormant in some individuals, while others may be taught from a young age to pay attention to it. I say "taught from a young age to pay attention to it" because I do believe that we are all are born with this ability. We just lose it over time when it is not acknowledged. At birth, we are closest to our true authentic selves, sans what we brought with us from past lives (if that is in your belief system), until or unless we decide to embark on a spiritual journey.

It would only make sense that if that theory is true, that if we have an ability to communicate with our Creator, then we would have it from infancy.

What do I mean by communication with your Creator? Do you hear voices? Very seldom is it the case that you would truly hear the voice of your Creator. It is much more subtle than a yelling voice or a crack of lightning followed by an earth-shattering message. True intuition is gentle, even when it is a warning. This may be one of the reasons it is often ignored. It is always comforting and never encourages you to harm yourself or anyone else. Think of the feeling you had when you were getting the most encouraging, loving advice you have ever received from any living person. Then multiply that feeling of comfort by about one hundred. That is what it feels like when you are truly tuned in to your intuition. It is guidance from your Creator. It is never self-serving, never jaded from life experiences, and always based on what you need in that moment.

Your intuition is at work all day long, guiding you to the right route to avoid traffic, telling you the food that your body needs, alerting you when a friend needs a phone call, or calling to you in many other situations. We often shrug some of the afore-mentioned examples off as "coincidences," but in reality as you begin to pay attention, you will notice that there truly is a reason for everything. It may be hard to understand why you would receive a message about something that is not more exciting than the examples given. It is easy to tell yourself that your Creator wouldn't bother with such trivi-al stuff. The truth is, if it is important to you, your Creator knows. There is nothing too trivial for you to receive intuition about.

Your intuition will guide you in whatever areas of your life need guidance at a particular moment, from what your body needs to major life changes, and even to what line might be quicker in the super-market. Some individuals receive guidance leading them to a career choice that would be more fulfill-ing than the one they are currently in.

Intuition is customized for you. It is not only the message you need to hear, but delivered in the way you need to hear it at the time that is right for you. That is also one of the reasons it can be so confusing.

It is different for everybody. Your Creator knows the most effective way for you to hear the message for you to stop and take notice of it, but there is not an owner's manual that gives you the meaning of every possible message you may receive. These messages are personal to each of us.

You will receive intuitive guidance through the impressions that you consider to be your strengths. Messages can be visual, auditory, kinesthetic, or you may just "know" something. Messages are frequently overlooked for one reason or another. Often this happens when we switch to thinking about our guidance instead of connecting to it. Just stop and be present. Pay attention to what is happening around you. Be aware of what your strengths are.

Your awareness of yourself will open you up to the manner in which your guidance is delivered. If you are somebody who tends to be visual, it would make sense for you to receive intuition through something that catches your eye like a billboard, television message, e-mail, or license plate, to give some examples. Some of you may have been called "know-it-alls" by others. Your guidance may be messages that you "know" without any real explanation of why. Others may need to hear something with their own ears for it to be real to them. You may hear a message in the form of a song when you turn on your radio or in a conversation that you overhear in public. Some individuals may have a strong sense of smell. Your nose may lead you to what you need to know when you smell a special aroma that conjures up a memory from the archives of your mind. Somebody who is kinesthetic may receive sensations in their body like gut feelings.

Regardless of the manner in which your guidance will be delivered, when you receive something that you think might be a message, stop and ask, "What does this mean or symbolize to me?" Your guidance will be meaningful to you based on your life experiences that make you who you are in the moment that you are receiving them. Intuition can and will use anything that makes sense to you. It can and will also be catered to you and to the number of times you may have ignored the message so far.

Everything you think is guidance will not be accurate at first. You may make mistakes, just like you do when you are developing any new skill. Just because everyone has this natural ability doesn't mean you will be ready to rely on your intuition for major life decisions right away. You won't, so please don't expect to! The majority of humans are born with the ability to run, but that does not mean they can run a marathon tomorrow if they have not trained for it. The same is true for intuition. If you haven't practiced using your intuition for the little decisions in your life that are inconsequential, you should not be making major life decisions based solely upon it.

Undeveloped intuition is no substitute for good old-fashioned common sense. Start with short distances; ask yourself insignificant questions like who is on the phone when it rings or how many e-mails will be awaiting you in your inbox when you log on to your computer in the morning, just by tuning in to your guidance. Keep a notebook of all the guidance you receive, including both the little stuff and the potential keys to overcoming your obstacles. You will get to know what it feels like to be truly tuned in the more you practice. Record everything you act on and those things you don't. Eventually, you will see a trend. Once you identify what it truly feels like to receive guidance, there will be no mistaking the feeling—the same way there is no mistaking other strong feelings once you feel them—like happiness or true love. Just find your inner barometer through trial and error.

One of the most difficult questions individuals have when they are first developing their intuition is how to distinguish whether they are making something up in their head or receiving true guidance. As mentioned, through practice your intuitive accuracy will grow. There are a few other distinguishing factors that may help as well. When you think something, it usually is based on your ego taking over. Ego-based messages will be personalized too, so be careful. Unlike guidance, ego-based messages can be negative in nature. If you have low self-esteem they can be self-deprecating at times. If you tend to have a high opinion of yourself, they can play on that with visions of grandeur. Intuition is balanced. It is relevant. It is positive, and it is clear. If a message is not clear, ask for clarity. Pay attention to how you feel, what you see, or notice when you receive messages. Individuals who are kinesthetic often say they receive chills as confirmation that they are receiving strong messages. Your Creator may have a special way of confirming messages for you too.

Although you receive guidance all day long, to gain clarity or tune in to your Creator more fully, meditate on the messages you think you are receiving. Take time to center yourself, as described in the steps given in Chapter 2 ("Tuning in to Your Spirit Through Meditative Practices"). Once you are at a place of stillness you will be more effective at determining what you are receiving, hearing, or seeing.

Intuition does not negate your need to take action. Your Creator allows you to have free will. You may receive a message over and over and know that it is important, but you may not take action. Your Creator will not force you to take action. The message may get clearer, repeat itself more often, and even increase in urgency. It will not do the work that you feel you need to do, though. If it is in your best interest to take a particular action, there is still a need on your part to be willing to help yourself. For example, if you are being guided to take better care of your body, you need to make the switch to a healthy diet and exercise program. Your Creator cannot do this for you.

There is always a need for balance. We need to act when we know it is appropriate, and stop and ask for guidance when things are not clear. We need to use sound judgment and understand that everything takes preparation. That also goes for the relay of our intuitive guidance and our understanding of it at times. You can receive clear guidance regarding a future goal, but you still need to follow the steps required to get you to the particular goal if you set your sights on acquiring it. If you have wanted to be a doctor since you were a child, you are probably meant to be a doctor, but you cannot become one without going to medical school first. We cannot do anything without preparation, so be clear on what it is that you are being guided to do, and be willing to take positive steps in order to achieve that which you desire.

Often you are given intuition in steps. You may get an overwhelming urge to go somewhere, learn something, or call somebody, but the reason for your action may not make sense at the time. We rarely get to see the whole big picture at one time. It is important to just tune in and ask yourself if the message is positive, without getting hung up on why you are being guided to take a certain action. You can meditate for clarity on what the guidance is, and when you are sure, take action. Your Creator knows you better than you do. He knows exactly what He needs to do to make you take action at just the right time and not a moment before. Each step will make sense when you arrive where you are being guided to go.

Regarding the clarity of the message you are receiving, your first impression is usually the closest to the true message. What did you immediately think, feel, hear, or know at a time when you felt or thought you were getting a message? Your level of accuracy will increase as you develop this ability, just as it will as you use the other tools in this book. The more you use the skill for little things, the more you will discover what it feels like to be tuned in. Take as long as you like to experiment. There is no race.

Following are some traits of true intuitive guidance:

1) It is always positive.

2) It will usually repeat itself when you do not take action at first—sometimes for years!

3) It feels comforting and loving in nature, even in a scary situation. (Example: "Go this way! It is safe!")

4) It *never* encourages you to harm yourself or anyone else.

5) It seems to be just what you need to hear, see, feel, or know at just the right time.

6) It will just *feel* right with your inner barometer.

With practice, you will develop your intuition. Take baby steps. Following is an exercise designed to get you to start tuning in to your internal GPS.

Exercise to Develop Your Intuition

1) Start by centering yourself as you do when you meditate. Once you get to a place of "stillness" by following the steps mentioned in Chapter 2 ("Tuning in to Your Spirit Through Meditative Practices"), ask yourself the questions listed below. Record your answers in a notebook after you receive your answer to each question. As you continue to practice, messages will flow more naturally.

2) Keep a notebook with a list of messages that you receive. Review them for accuracy at a later date.

3) Get used to what it feels like to be right by asking for guidance on insignificant issues like:

   a) What is the best way to go to work so my commute is as smooth as possible today?

b) What menu item would I most enjoy (at a specific restaurant that you may not be familiar with)?

c) Which restaurant should I go to (if you are unfamiliar with the area)?

d) Where will I find a parking spot (in a crowded parking lot)?

e) Who is on the telephone? (When the phone rings, ask this without looking at caller ID.)

f) Which line will get me checked out the fastest (in a supermarket)?

g) Where can I find this product at the most affordable price? (You can confirm this by comparison shopping afterward.)

Get used to what it really feels like to be tuned in by practicing with some of the questions mentioned in the previous exercise. Use some of your own questions of similarly low importance. Don't start out with important questions like whether or not to buy a home or quit your job. It takes time to develop this skill. Develop it to your comfort or motivation level. Some may decide they want to develop it to a high level of accuracy. Others may be satisfied with just knowing who is on the phone when it rings.

Not everyone who develops their intuition to a level of high accuracy is meant to be a spiritual teacher. Balance any motivation to help others with the temptation to run from society. Remember, intuition is meant to give you guidance through your life. Any messages that you receive for others are secondary. Practice assimilating your new tool, your internal GPS, into your existing life. I used my intuition when I worked in corporate America to do sales forecasts every quarter. If you do not have a highly developed skill set, I don't recommend that you do this--I did, so I was able to benefit from it. I was often rewarded for the accuracy of my forecasting, and my supervisors never knew how I came up with the numbers other than what I showed them on spreadsheets to support it. There was no reason for me to share that it was based on my gut feelings.

As you learn to adjust to using your internal GPS in your life, pay attention to those things that you may have always taken for granted—those things you just know. No matter where I am, even if I am out of the country, if my best friend leaves me a message at home without my knowledge, I get the urge to call her within moments. She remarked one day that she feels like she doesn't even have to call me anymore. All she has to do is think of me, and she knows the phone will ring—and it does. Maybe you have a connection like this with somebody as well. This is your intuition letting you know that your special connection is reaching out to you.

Intuition can also show itself through a feeling in the pit of your stomach, causing you to avoid someone, despite the lack of any logical reason or wrong-doing on anyone's part. You might think in a case like this that "he or she seems nice, but something just doesn't feel right." If you ignore your guidance, you may soon find that the individual was not as nice as they seemed at all. Intuition might also show up as an instant connection with someone you meet for the first time. Later, you find your guidance to be correct because the person you were drawn to ends up being one of your closest friends. The examples are endless, and yours may differ from others.

Although your intuition can be subtle at times, tuning in to it is valuable. I had a student who was distressed because she believed she never heard from her guides. I reassured her that she just needed to listen more fully. That evening during a group meditation, she heard the club mix of "Hymn" by 4 Clubbers while listening to one of my playlists. It was a song of relevance in her life, but she only heard it as a result of my playlist "malfunctioning." This song certainly wasn't on my meditation playlist, and I didn't even know it was on my iPod. I'd never heard it before, but she loved it!

After her special song finished, it looped and played again. It stopped only after I interrupted the class and asked who the message was for, and she explained what this music meant to her. Until then, I'd never had issues with my iPod. But from that day forward, whenever that student came to class, she'd be given messages through my music. After the class was completed, my music setup went back to normal. It no longer changed itself—that is, until I had another student who had his or her own special connection to music.

The point is to start paying attention. Notice those ideas that seem to come to you consistently. If your Creator is trying to get your attention, He will repeat Himself when you are not listening. If you are drawn to something, begin to ask why. Don't ever think you or something in your life are not important enough for you to receive guidance. If you are unsure, stop and ask for clarification. You are establishing a connection that allows you to give and receive communication. Just like with the other tools mentioned in this book, start gradually, taking baby steps, and build with your comfort level.

4~Being Your Authentic Self

It takes a lot of effort to be someone else. As you tune in to your soul and once again connect to your Creator, you'll learn the importance of being yourself. Many self-help gurus suggest looking at qualities in people you admire and acting like them. Instead, I suggest discovering *who you truly are* and being yourself. That doesn't mean that you should ignore a quality you see in yourself that you admire in somebody else. It just means there is no need to compare yourself to anyone else! When you uncover who you truly are, you will find that you have qualities that make you admirable that will allow your spirit to shine. Some people spend so much energy trying to be someone they aren't that they become exhausted. They copy others' mannerisms, hair, dress, slang, and so on. Some even take others' work and claim it as their own, all in an effort to be somebody they are not. If they don't have the same success or the success they feel they have "earned" from all of "their" hard work, they feel cheated.

When you remember that each and every one of us has a purpose for being here and you are given your own unique natural abilities to carry it out, you will realize that there is no need to copy somebody else's work because what you are meant to do with your own abilities will give you recognition. That recognition will far surpass that of any received from copying another. If you try to mimic the work or manner of another, it will come off as inauthentic. Others may not verbalize it, but they just know something is not quite *right*, so you will often not get the results you expect.

At times individuals may copy the actions of their teachers, friends, or even celebrities they view as more successful than they are. It can be an effort to reach a level of financial security or to achieve the life that they interpret the other has. If they're effectively *imitating* someone, they are crossing energetic boundaries.

What are energetic boundaries? Energetic boundaries are boundaries that are most often not marked like your personal property but just understood. Although some stay constant with everyone, others will vary depending on the depths of the relationship. An example of these boundaries is our personal space in talking to somebody. You feel a violation of your personal space much more profoundly if a stranger, rather than your spouse or mate, leans in to get close to you. Energetic boundaries can be extended to things you take ownership of that often are not of a material nature, like slang you use, phrases you become known for, great ideas you develop, or a particular style that you have about you that makes you unique.

The fact that you are not taking something physically, does not mean you are not crossing boundaries. Before now, you may not have been able to put your finger on the strange feeling you have gotten when you are around somebody you notice is trying to imitate you, but you may now remember that it just *felt* weird. It *felt* weird to you because your energetic boundaries were being crossed, and that does not *feel* good to anyone. Although the individuals cannot really ever "take" another's personality or success the way material property can be taken, if you have ever experienced this, you know it feels like a violation—or, at the very least, for most of us it feels like a grave crossing of our social boundaries. We will talk more about boundaries in Chapter 9 ("Teaching Others How to Treat You").

We are all human, so it is understandable that we will all have some kind of similarity, but acknowledge when the similarities are genuine versus an attempt to be someone you're not. Be honest with yourself about if you share a quality or gift with somebody and want to develop it or if you are imitating him or her. If the distinction is not clear to you, ask yourself if you are aspiring to be more like others because of a trait or skill they hold or if you catch yourself wanting to *be* somebody else. Remember, we were all given gifts to help us to fulfill our life's purpose. If you are acting inauthentically, chances are you are not fulfilling your life's purpose. Stop and ask yourself why you're doing what you are doing. Ask yourself if you are really being true to who you are. When you do something that isn't authentic, you won't find peace. This is not a "punishment"; it is just a law of the universe. When you push yourself to be somebody you are not, your soul will recognize this and make every effort to get you back on track. If you are trying to block the message, you may feel like it is a negative emotion. Sometimes, rather than sadness or the like, negative emotions are just our body-mind-spirit's way of encouraging us to be ourselves.

If this could be you, if you're willing to expend that much energy, why not develop your own natural talents and abilities? You are here for your own specific purpose, to carry out your own specific plan in your own unique way. Take advantage of the gifts you were born with. That's what the Creator meant for *you*. Here is a little secret—it takes less effort too!

Even though everyone is the best they can be when they are their own authentic self, it can be difficult to determine who that is. Your authentic self is who you are, stripped of any negative emotions. The real you is who you are on the inside: your soul.

It is every good quality that you hold—hidden or seen. It is the whisper deep inside that makes you question if there is more to life than just existing. It is what motivates you to read books like this.

Let's strip some of the armor away and see what is on the inside. Answer these questions to help you meet the real you. When answering them, remove yourself from your responses as much as possible and answer the questions as if you were answering on behalf of your dearest friend.

Example:

Introducing...You!

1) What have you always wanted to do ever since you could remember?

be a teacher

2) What did you love to do as a child?

play "school," play with dolls, and swim

3) What are you passionate about?

children who are in need

4) What would you do if you didn't have to make money?

teach

5) What qualities do you value most in a person?

honesty, integrity, hard work, being a good friend

6) What is the highest compliment you have ever received from somebody else?

You made me believe in myself.

Introducing... You!

1) What have you always wanted to do ever since you could remember?

_____

_____

2) What did you love to do as a child?

_____

_____

3) What are you passionate about?

_____

_____

4) What would you do if you didn't have to make money?

_____

_____

5) What qualities do you value most in a person?

_____

_____

6) What is the highest compliment you have ever received from somebody else?

_____

_____

Now that you have answered the questions, review your answers to see what you have always been passionate about.

Looking at your achievements over the years can remind you of your accomplishments and also what you are passionate about working toward. As you list your achievements, big or small, you will learn what motivates you and begin to see your amazing triumphs.

Example:

What are your top twenty achievements?

(Even if you don't think your accomplishments are significant, list them. Start with yesterday and go back as far as you can remember.)

1. Purchasing my own home

2. Receiving my college degree

3. Becoming a fitness trainer

4. Competing in the state championship in high school

5. Getting three promotions in fewer than ten years

6. Learning to dance

7. Purchasing my first new car on my own

8. Completing a triathlon

9. Receiving an award for being in the top 10 percent of my company

10. Paying off my first car

11. Paying off my first home

12. Having perfect attendance in college

13. Getting initiated into a leadership honor society in college

14. Saving a drowning person

15. Learning to water ski

16. Learning to snow ski

17. Increasing my territory by 80 percent in one year

18. Exceeding team goals by 10 to 20 percent each year

19. Being promoted to manager at the store where I worked during college

20. Losing ten pounds and keeping them off

What are your top twenty highest achievements?

(Even if you don't think they are significant, list them.)

1. _____

2. _____

3. _____

4. _____

5. _____

6. _____

7. _____

8. _____

9. _____

10. _____

11. _____

12. _____

13. _____

14. _____

15. _____

16. _____

17. _____

18. _____

19. _____

20. _____

Now that you have listed your accomplishments, review them. Look at the things you have always enjoyed working towards.

Creating a bucket list allows you to remove the limits you may have put on your life and to live with passion. Think about the things you have said you always wanted to do but just keep putting off.

Example:

Build a bucket list of at least 20 things.

(What are 20 things you want to do in your lifetime?)

1. Run a marathon

2. Learn to play the saxophone

3. Get a pilot's license

4. Travel across the country

5. Not check e-mail for forty-eight hours

6. Experience a true lasting romantic relationship

7. Go see the Olympics

8. Travel to my childhood vacation spot again

9. Complete a triathlon

10. Travel to Italy

11. Go on a picnic in France

12. Have champagne and fondue in front of a fireplace in a snowed-in getaway

13. Watch the sunset in each of the seven continents

14. Visit the temples of Japan

15. Ski in Whistler

16. Take a sailing lesson

17. Help feed the hungry at a homeless shelter

18. Kiss my true love in the pouring rain

19. Study Yoga with one of the great masters

20. Get a master's degree

Build a bucket list of at least 20 things.

(What are 20 things you want to do in your lifetime?)

1. _____

2. _____

3. _____

4. _____

5. _____

6. _____

7. _____

8. _____

9. _____

10. _____

11. _____

12. _____

13. _____

14. _____

15. _____

16. _____

17. _____

18. _____

19. _____

20. _____

Review the information that you recorded about yourself. Look at it as if you are meeting yourself for the first time. Take time to see what really makes you tick. Take time to see who you truly are inside and what you are passionate about. Examine what you would choose to do if you could remove all the "can'ts." Look at what makes you unique. There are no coincidences. You weren't born with talents or natural abilities just so you could waste them. You have a niche! Discover yours and run with it. That's when you'll truly shine; that's when you'll perform at your best.

In fact, that's the secret to the success and happiness of many of those you admire. They're already being who they are.

5~If Life Isn't Going Your Way, Change It!

The Law of Attraction says that *like attracts like.* Some refer to this as the "law of the universe." Whatever you call it, the old adage applies: You get what you focus on.-If there's something in your life you don't like, change it by applying the Law of Attraction. Life doesn't *happen to you.* The only one in charge of your life is you!

Examine your life and break it down into various components. At this moment, consider in which areas you desire change: finances, relationships, family, environment, career, friends, health, or something else. Even given your blind spots (those areas that may feel *off* but never struck you as things you wanted to change), do your best to look at your life as realistically as you can.

To uncover your blind spots, examine the areas you *didn't* mention, yet you spend countless hours complaining about. You might turn green with envy when you see others with what you perceive as strengths. You might spend innumerable hours worrying about these areas and letting them make you feel bad about yourself. Congratulations! You've identified the stagnant areas of your life—blind spots—where you weren't aware that you wanted change. Identifying these themes is half the battle.

After uncovering areas in which you desire change, be a *truth-seeker* of your desires, and make them your reality. Remember, you are in control. At every moment, you have the opportunity to be positive or negative about what happens around you. When you make any decision, your perspective is matched by the Law of Attraction. For example, if you've always struggled with money, you may have developed a negative association with money. It is almost as if you develop a habit of associating with money negatively. It is imperative that you change your perspective on money in a positive way. A negative viewpoint will work as a roadblock to getting what you desire. Eliminating these learned obstacles clears the way for you to receive that which you desire. That's how you'll attract what you want into your life.

This approach may feel unnatural at first, but that's to be expected when you are changing a habit. As you consciously change patterns you have created, know that you have to give up what no longer serves you. You may have grown up hearing "If you want to get ahead, you have to work hard." You have always worked hard and made this your mantra from childhood, yet you see many of your peers getting ahead of you and putting in far less effort. What if you changed this belief to "Work smarter, not harder"?

Others may be successful in their careers but have termed themselves "unlucky in love" due to their dating experiences in the past. What if those individuals were able to shift to believing that there is somebody out there for everyone and that they are "holding out for the right one"? Do you see how you feel different when you read the different perspectives?

The good news is that just like working out pays off by bringing you to the fitness level you desire, consciously making an effort to send out positive messages will bring you the life you desire.

I have included exercises to help you get started. I encourage you to try all of these exercises to flex your Law of Attraction muscle. That's how you'll begin to discover what you truly desire—and attain it!

How to Uncover What You Want

1) Make a collage. Go through old magazines and cut out everything that catches your eye. When you are done, look at each thing you cut out and ask yourself if that is something you desire in your life. Create a collage of all the things to which you say "yes." You're creating an image of the life you intend to build. Display this collage somewhere you can see it every day.

2) Close your eyes and picture your life as you would like to see it. Imagine how it would look, feel, sound, and even smell if everything you desire was in your life. Feel the way that you would feel, knowing that you have created this aspect of your life just as you want it. Look at how your life would appear in vivid color. Imagine what those who support you would say about your

accomplishments. Let your imagination take you wherever you want it to go. Take yourself back to your daydreaming days, but do it with the purpose of achieving all of your desires. After you are done, write a list of all the desires that you uncovered in the space provided.

3) You can use extra sheets of paper if you run out of room. List everything that you notice is important to you, even if you already have it in your life. List everything as if you have already achieved your goals or desires. If you make the statement believable to yourself, you will shift your energy to be in alignment with obtaining that which you desire.

Example:

Desires: Things that you are actively working to achieve or maintain.

(Some may call these goals.)

1) I am slim, fit, and healthy.

2) I have a loving family.

3) I am helping others.

4) Others appreciate me for what I do.

5) I have a loving spouse.

6) I have two adorable loving children.

7) My career is rewarding and allows me to give back.

8) I am well compensated for the work that I do.

9) I pay my bills easily, with money left over for savings and donations.

10) I have a job that allows me to work from home at times.

11) I have a flexible schedule.

12) I am able to easily fit work and "me time" into my schedule.

13) I enjoy athletic events in my downtime.

14) I work for an ethical company that treats its employees well.

15) I have many close friends who share my interests.

Desires: Things that you are actively working to achieve or maintain.

(Some may call these goals.)

1)_____

2)_____

3)_____

4)_____

5)_____

6)_____

7)_____

8)_____

9)_____

10)_____

11)_____

12)_____

13)_____

14)_____

15)_____

Now that you are closer to knowing what you want, let's put a holistic approach to the old Law of Attraction theory. You often put limits on what you attract, with your own specifics of what you think you want. Although having clarity is important, staying open to even better options is equally important.

Let me give you an example. Suppose one of your desires is to own a home on a lake. You may have a lake in mind, but there may be a better fit for your needs that you don't know about. If you focus only on that particular lake rather than all of the lakes that exist in the desired geographic location, you create obstacles to manifesting your desire for a lake house.

Maybe you would like to adopt a child from abroad. You could begin your search generally until guided to streamline it to a specific location. If you start out too specific, you could employ a much more limited search than you should and end up missing the child that was meant for you at first.

Do you get the idea? The broader generalization allows you to put your desires out there, without the limitations that may be set by a focus that is too specific. When you look at things in a more general sense and are open to your Creator guiding you to what is dedicated to your highest good, you will manifest what is truly best suited for you. That is when you will be guided to your heart's desires.

Following are some tips to help you to navigate toward manifesting your best life.

A Holistic Approach to the Law of Attraction

1) Tune in to your needs.

2) What you think you "want" is not always what is dedicated to your highest good.

3) Sometimes we need to be open to manifesting something that is better suited for us in place of our intended desire. Practice being open to receiving something equal to or even better than imagined.

4) We are often given "hints" of what is better suited for us, almost in a nagging way. Tune in to those "hints" and they will direct you to what is meant for you.

5) Do you often have nagging reminders of something that you "talk yourself out of"?

   • If so, what are you being reminded of?

   • What does it mean?

   • If you don't know, meditate and ask for guidance.

   • When you are confident, move ahead.

6~Manifesting Your Desires and Guarding Your Mood Through the Process

Once you determine what you want, it's important to be mindful of the words you choose and the conversations in which you participate. This will help you to guard your mood from outside influences. When you talk to family, friends or co-workers, their energy may catch you in its wake. It's noble to want to be the person that's always there for your friends, but you don't grow by listening to other people's sad stories and making them your own. The next time you want to be *there* for somebody, try lifting their spirits instead of joining them in their misery.

Protect your mood from internal conflict caused by your own thoughts or emotions. You are human. Sometimes you will have negative thoughts. I encourage you to be mindful of how often you allow yourself to have thoughts that have a negative effect on your mood. Do what you can to remain positive, and prevent a negative shift from occurring whenever possible. If you catch yourself feeling down, be proactive and do what you can to lift your mood by partaking in an activity that you know raises your spirit. Simple acts like turning on music, smelling a nice fresh scent, or taking a walk are examples of activities that may help you shift from feeling down to feeling happy. What you choose to do is not as important as selecting something that has the ability to lift your mood, whatever that may be for you.

With a little planning, you will find yourself working less at lifting your mood. Individuals may have difficulty remaining positive if they don't have anything to look forward to on a regular basis. It's easy to get in a rut if your job has become mundane and you are too bogged down with all of the other demands of life. It is important to have something that you want to get out of bed for in the morning. If you feel like your life lacks excitement, zest, passion, or drive, decide today that you will do something that you look forward to every day. It doesn't matter if it is for ten minutes or two hours. Find something that you want to do for yourself, put it on your calendar, and make it a priority. It doesn't have to be the same thing every day as long as there is something you can look forward to when you get up each morning.

Actively work at staying positive. At first this may feel like work, but as you continue you will find it coming more naturally. People use a variety of tools to stay positive. One of those tools is a mantra. A mantra is a phrase that you say over and over with the intention of manifesting or bringing about what that phrase means to you. It is important to use one that resonates with you. It doesn't have to be eloquent or profound; it just has to embody whatever you are intending to manifest or create in your life. It also needs to relate personally to you. Sometimes it isn't what's said, but how it's said and the feeling behind it.

As you are forming or adopting a mantra of your own, make sure it is believable to you. Saying things that don't *feel right* to you doesn't serve you. You are doing more harm than good. For example, if your intention is to manifest financial abundance, you might adopt a mantra like "I easily pay my bills each month with an excess of money remaining." But if every time you say it, your mind says to itself, "Yeah, right!" accompanied by a vision of bouncing checks, it would be more effective if you made the statement more believable to you. Don't focus only on what you are saying but on how you feel when you are saying it and the images that are conjured up in your mind. Change your words to something like "I am creating a shift in my life in regard to..." or whatever works for you. In the case of our example of financial abundance, perhaps a phrase more like "I am making a shift to financial freedom that will allow me to pay all of my bills each month and have money left over" would feel better to you. This statement may be more easily believable to you, and it implies that you aren't there yet but are creating a shift to get there. Do you notice how the feeling changes when you read the two different statements?

This is your life. Don't wait for it to get better. Take a proactive approach to creating the life you desire while enjoying each moment along the way. Start loving your life today. You owe it to yourself.

The idea is for you to increase your positivity a little more each day. If you wobble a little, it's okay. Stick with it; take baby steps. The moment you catch yourself being negative or feeling defeated, make a decision to turn things around. The following questions can help you to identify areas where you may want to begin making changes.

Example:

Questions:

1) How often do you schedule something that you enjoy?

Possible answer: Twice a year.

Homework—I will schedule something I enjoy on my calendar every day. (This can be different daily but should be scheduled ahead of time.)

Possible choice: I will go for a ten-minute walk in the woods to clear my head after work.

2) How often do you feel good when you get up in morning?

Possible answer: Never

Homework—In preparation for the next day, I will plan something special for myself the night before.

(What would make your morning easier? More pleasant?)

Possible choice: I will set up the coffee-pot so it is ready the night before. I love freshly brewed coffee!

Questions:

1) How often do you schedule something that you enjoy?

_____

_____

Homework—I will schedule something I enjoy on my calendar every day. (This can be different daily but should be scheduled ahead of time.)

_____

_____

2) How often do you feel good when you get up in morning?

_____

_____

Homework—In preparation for the next day, I will plan something special for myself the night before.

(What would make your morning easier? More pleasant?)

_____

_____

True/False Questions to Identify Your Blind Spots:

1) I have a satisfying romantic relationship. T/F

2) I love my career. I do something I am passionate about. T/F

3) I have good friends with whom I spend time regularly. T/F

4) My home environment makes me feel at ease. T/F

5) I have enough money to afford my expenses easily. T/F

If you answered "False" to any of the questions and you haven't recognized it as representing an area that you would like to work on, it is a blind spot for you. Go back and determine what you do want.

Working with the energy of the universe can leave you feeling like an actor who doesn't know his or her lines. It can appear that things come out of nowhere at times, leaving you with a feeling of being unprepared. Sometimes it leaves you scratching your head wondering what happened. There are people and situations that you may not even be aware of that can sabotage your perspective along the way. I refer to these things as *vibe killers* because they affect your vibrations within the universe. As you review these *vibe killers*, you may find that the same people and events seem to deplete your energy frequently. When you are aware of them, you will be in a better position to protect your mood and energy from them. Then you will see that the mood changes you experience are a direct result of who and what you interact with on a daily basis.

Keep a running total throughout the day of the things that deflate your mood. You will begin to notice a trend of who and what the main culprits are. *Vibe killers* are areas of your life that you may consider tough obligations. They take the energy out of you, but for one reason or another you tell yourself, "You have to…" Until you start to critically think about them, you may not notice the area or individual(s) draining your energy. These are people you want to prepare for if they must remain in your life.

Come up with a plan ahead of time for how you can get those people to join you in your good mood rather than pull you into their misery. If you know somebody that has this effect on you, it becomes easier to be around them once you prepare. You begin to recognize the other person's hot buttons. You know that even if these people are miserable 95 percent of the time, there is 5 percent when they are happy. Use this knowledge to your advantage. Help them to increase their 5 percent. You don't have to tell them what you are doing. It doesn't have to turn into a lesson on the Law of Attraction every time you see them. Just use your knowledge to shift them into a better mood, thereby protecting your own in the process. Even if these people don't know it, staying in that negative mood doesn't serve them either.

Learn to guard your *vibe* like a precious treasure. You are in charge. You decide how you do or don't react to others and their situations. If something affects your mood negatively, be aware of it. Your goal in the next exercise is to identify the areas and people in your life that affect your mood negatively and to create a plan to protect your mood in the future. Throughout a single day, simply record each thing, event, or person that causes you to feel drained, or when you notice your mood feels depleted on the worksheet provided. For more clarification, you can continue the exercise for a longer period of time.

Example:

"Vibe Killers"—Things, Events, and Individuals that Bring My Mood Down

1) Negative e-mails from my boss

2) My friend Suzie, who calls me daily, with drama during my lunch hour

3) Traffic

4) My co-workers gossiping about one another

5) Unnecessary interruptions while I am working

6) My mom calling to criticize me about how we raise our children

7) Dinner always being rushed

8) Having to fight to get my kids to do homework

9) Never having anyone help out with after-dinner cleanup

10) Having to fight to get the kids to bed at night and then up in the morning

"Vibe Killers"—Things, Events, and Individuals that Bring My Mood Down

1) _____

2) _____

3) _____

4) _____

5) _____

6) _____

7) _____

8) _____

9) _____

10) _____

Review "Vibe Killers"

Who or what are your vibe killers?

1) Which can you avoid? Is it necessary to have them in your life?

2) How can you bring them up to your level or encourage a more pleasant experience?

Alternatively, you will run across things that lift your mood for the better. Take notice of those people or things too. You will see that just as some people seem to steal your positive vibration, others lift your vibration repeatedly. These are the people you want to have in your life. They make shifting to a more positive life effortless for you.

Let's identify those individuals or situations that are your *vibe thrillers*. A great way of intentionally bringing up your vibe is to remember those things in your life that make you smile no matter what. Everyone's list will be different and personal to them, but recalling the things that are constant sources of joy can help you turn things around when you are feeling down. Your goal is to allow your vibe to remain positive as much as possible.

Throughout a single day, simply record on the provided worksheet each thing, event, or person that causes you to feel happy, along with times when you notice that your mood feels energized. For more clarification, you can continue the exercise for a longer period of time.

Example:

"Vibe Thrillers"—Things, Events, and Individuals that I Am Thankful For

1) My coffee was ready when I got up in the morning.

2) Somebody let me merge in front of them in a line of traffic.

3) My department got free lunch today.

4) Mark, my co-worker, always appreciates my hard work.

5) My husband picked up dinner.

6) My son hit a home run at school today.

7) My daughter got an A on her spelling test.

8) The sunrise was beautiful this morning.

9) I love listening to good music on my commute!

10) I am able to return calls during my commute.

11) My dog always greets me so happily when I get home.

12) My kids are always excited to tell me about their day.

13) My husband gives the best hugs ever when he arrives home.

14) I love the jokes and fun during family dinner-time.

"Vibe Thrillers"—Things, Events, and Individuals that I Am Thankful For

1) _____

2) _____

3) _____

4) _____

5) _____

6) _____

7) _____

8) _____

9) _____

10) _____

11) _____

12) _____

13) _____

14) _____

Review Vibe Thrillers:

1) Who/what are your vibe thrillers?

2) How can you incorporate them into your life more?

Know yourself and know what you can do that lifts your mood. Some suggestions are reading a great book, reciting an inspirational quote or mantra, using good scents (candles, oils, etc.), moving your body by—exercising or listening to music, and remembering your *vibe thrillers* or anything else that lifts your spirit.

Other ideas that may raise your vibe/ mood

1) Read books.

2) Write great quotes on note cards so you can find them.

3) Cut out things that make you smile.

4) Use great scents: scented candles, essential oils, etc.

5) Move: exercise, go outside, dance, stand up out of your chair

6) Listen to uplifting music.

Once we begin using the energy of the universe, we will notice that we can manifest our desires just as easily as we can manifest the negative things we focus on. When we learn to apply the same principles used to manifest the desires we already have, we continue bringing the desires we wish for into our reality.

7~Identifying Your Patterns to Unlock the Code to Manifesting the Life You Desire

Throughout your life, you will develop patterns that can help you or distract you from manifesting your desires. By patterns I mean themes throughout your life, positive or negative, that seem to repeat themselves. We can develop patterns through our actions, roles we adopt or are "given," or other means. Often we just come to accept these archetypes as "truths" whether or not they serve us.

When I was a teenager, shortly after I got my driver's license, I was pulled over and given a speeding ticket. From that point on, every time I was pulled over I was given a speeding ticket. I expected it, and that is exactly what happened. One day, I said, "This is ridiculous. It's time to change this story," so I did. I made a conscious decision to change the story that I was telling about being pulled over and getting speeding tickets. No sooner did I make this decision than I came across somebody standing in front of a store asking for donations to benefit a local police league. Prior to that moment, I was immediately intimidated by police officers when I came across them. This time, I noticed, was completely different. The feeling was positive from the moment I saw the individual. Without any explanation needed, I just smiled and made a donation, knowing my intention of wiping my slate clean had already occurred. Thank goodness!

A popular area to develop these patterns is within the relationships we have with others. Have you ever met somebody who hasn't worked through the emotional trauma attached to a divorce or breakup? Often these individuals are quick to overshare their story of being "screwed over" to any sympathetic ear willing to listen. Some are only too happy to leave a path of carnage everywhere they go saying how *relationships won't last*. Although being hurt by another that you trusted is hard, adopting the story and retelling it only keeps the story alive for you to relive it over and over in each relationship that you experience.

If you have had tough relationships in the past, observe other relationships that have the characteristics you would like. Notice that they are out there and that they do exist. You may experience very loving relationships with your family and friends but only experience the block within romantic relationships. Acknowledge that if it is out there for others and you are experiencing it in platonic relationships, then of course you can experience it in romantic ones, too!

Others may develop patterns in their careers— either positive or negative. Have you ever met somebody who just *seems to have things fall into place* everywhere they go? It doesn't matter where they go or what they try professionally; it seems like they not only excel but are rewarded. These individuals can serve as the object of our jealousy or motivation to get moving if we are not experiencing the same truth. If asked their secret, these same individuals often say that they just always thought they would get ahead, and they do.

Following are some pointers to help you identify patterns that you may have developed in your life.

- Look at the areas of your life that are positive. What do these accomplishments have in common?

- How do you speak about that area of your life?

- Remember, it's not only about what you say, but more importantly it's about how you feel about what you say.

- We create blockages and obstacles in our own lives with the *stories* we tell.

- If something isn't working, change your belief system. It isn't serving you. Why would you want to keep it?

- Are you prepared to let go of what isn't serving you?

Over time we can develop patterns in our lives that will affect our ability to manifest our desires, both positive and negative. If they are positive patterns, they will help us manifest our desires. If they are negative patterns, they can create obstacles.

If you have always considered yourself to be lucky, you may expect the positive results to continue. Maybe you have always won sweepstakes or local drawings. On the contrary, if you have always entered contests and never won, you might continue to expect that outcome.

As mentioned, some people develop patterns with their careers or relationships. Others can create these patterns with their self-image. Were you always seen as a shy, overweight kid without a voice and now, despite being a successful professional, you still tell yourself that you just aren't athletic and can't lose weight? Have you always been the athlete in your family and, therefore, seen as the *competitive one* in the family? Sometimes we outgrow our roles yet still see ourselves as the same—perpetuating a false, deprecating self-image.

The next exercise was designed to assist you in identifying the patterns that you may have developed in your own life.

- Without judgment, look for patterns, titles, and roles you have in your life.

- Once you have identified these patterns, titles, and roles, decide if they are helping you to achieve your desires.

- If they aren't, be willing to let go of them. Learn the lesson by looking at the events as an observer. Then let them go.

- Make changes in your life by changing your behavior.

Example:

What patterns (and even titles and roles) do you have in your life?

1) son- Y

2) father- Y

3) husband- Y

4) mentor- Y

5) director- Y

6) coach- Y

7) nephew- Y

8) friend- Y

9) grandson- Y

10) neighbor- Y

11) helper or "fix-it guy"- Y

12) pushover- N

13) athlete- Y

14) brother- Y

15) family "loan officer"- N

What patterns (and even titles and roles) do you have in your life?

1) _____

2) _____

3) _____

4) _____

5) _____

6) _____

7) _____

8) _____

9) _____

10) _____

11) _____

12) _____

13) _____

14) _____

15) _____

Go back to your list and decide if each item is having a positive impact on your life. Mark each one with a "Y" for "Yes" or "N" for "No."

Now that you have gone through the exercises in this chapter, you are probably starting to notice a shift in your life already. You will continue to notice that your life will blossom as you begin to allow the tools that you have obtained while reading this book to work with the laws of the universe to manifest your desires and create a life that is filled with joy, passion, and peace. As you go through the process, be kind to yourself. Go through each exercise, giving it the time you are guided to take and then moving on. Have a sense of humor with yourself, with the quirks that you may uncover, and feel a sense of accomplishment for what you have already achieved prior to and during this process. Once you learn these tools, they are yours for your lifetime. As your needs and desires change, you now have the tools to adapt to those changes.

8~Dealing with Life's Disappointments

Throughout your life you will have disappointments like being passed over for a promotion, ending relationships, having people be unkind to you, or dealing with other situations that are out of your control.

When faced with disappointments due to another's actions, remember the laws of the universe are always at work. Wanting to get even is a waste of energy and generates bad karma for you. Be content, knowing nobody can hide from karma. There are no free rides.

So do what you will. Say what you must. Steal. Cheat. Lie. Just know your actions will come back to you in some form; it's only a matter of time. This is not a threat, just the Law of Karma.

Therefore, don't waste your time with negative feelings about what somebody said or did. Set your boundaries clearly, feel what you feel, and trust that there's absolutely nothing you need to do. Also, trust that if there are lessons others need to learn, they will get more opportunities; that is certain.

I am human. I have gotten angry when I've been hurt by others. When I find my anger is getting the best of me, I make a point to remember that the actions of others create their own karma and if I choose to retaliate, it affects mine. At the end of any situation, good or bad, our actions will have consequences. It is up to you if you would like those consequences to be positive or negative. If it is in my best interest to hold somebody accountable, rather than lash out, I can do it without speaking harsh words. I'm no longer willing to allow somebody who mistreats me to take anything more from me. That means guarding my karma by being conscious of the way I react.

Did you ever notice that when you react negatively—even if the conflict is justified—you end up feeling as bad as the person you're in a disagreement with? Being human, we can all draw upon a memory of when we lashed out before we took a moment to breathe and collect our thoughts. It may have been snapping at your spouse after he or she left dishes in the sink, your response to a friend who decided to post what you viewed as the worst pictures he or she could find of you for all of your contacts to see on a social media site, your colleague who said something that unintentionally hurt your feelings, or your child who didn't listen to your multiple requests to behave.

When we are faced with reacting to an unpleasant circumstance, the varying harshness of situations can challenge us to remember to mind our karma. It is much easier to overlook others' unkind words or actions if they are merely acquaintances, leaving any thoughts of retaliation in the hands of karma, than it is to do so with somebody you have a close bond with. I often hear of individuals who, when faced with proof of their partner's infidelity, decide to do the same in retaliation. In the end, the first partner was wrong to begin with, and now the wronged partner feels even worse. The wronged partner places themselves in a position of also being a cheating spouse, lessening their self-worth. If that person had just stopped, gathered his or her thoughts, and told the spouse about being aware of the betrayal, the two could calmly decide the next course for the relationship—whether they choose to seek counseling or to dissolve it. It is not a question of whether or not we have a right to be annoyed. Sometimes we have a right to be downright *pissed off*. The question is how we choose to voice our disappointment.

Others have shared that since they were passed over for a promotion that they felt they deserved, they have not been putting in an honest day's work. Has anything like this occurred in your life? If it has, remember that if you were not recognized when you were working hard for your company, you are certainly making sure you won't be recognized for your hard work if you don't do it. Stop and decide if the job you have is worth keeping, and if so, work hard to get the next promotion that is available. Wouldn't it be a good idea to let your boss know that you were disappointed that you were not given the promotion, but you will be working hard to ensure the next one that opens up is offered to you?

Do you see how you can turn situations around just by stopping and considering your next step instead of acting out of haste?

Perhaps some of these examples resonate with you, or maybe they invoke other memories within your own life. The message is this: discussing something rather than yelling or retaliating in a negative manner doesn't mean that what another did was okay. It just means that you won't allow the other's behavior to rob you of your peace.

Choosing to handle a negative situation with someone peacefully doesn't mean that the other will be pleased with what you have to say. Sometimes you are still faced with having difficult discussions. I've had civilized conversations in which I told people their behavior was unacceptable to me. Consequently, there are a small handful of people I have had to say were no longer welcome in my life. I didn't resort to name-calling or yelling. I calmly stuck to the facts and wished them well. It wasn't ever my intention to put them in their place or get even. Rather, I had to hold them accountable when they crossed boundaries that I had set too many times. Check in with your inner barometer to assess if particular relationships are salvageable based on the circumstances.

Karma isn't a punishment system; it's a lesson. If you're inflicting harm on others, there is a lesson missing that your soul needs in order to help it to get to the next level. When a lesson is big enough and we are devoid of its moral, we can act out of desperation, often unaware of the limitless nature of all that surrounds us. At the same time, when you treat others well and expect nothing in return, that is recognized, too. You'll be rewarded in karmic currency.

Have you ever met somebody who is miserable to everyone he or she meets, yet can't figure out why nothing goes his or her way? These people are the first to update everyone in the area of all disasters existing on their continent, they have a reason for disliking virtually every race that exists except their own, and you can't remember the last time he or she even smiled. The same individuals may be the last to volunteer to help anyone else. They have never donated even so much as a dollar to the needy, but forever complain of their being screwed by the world. This description may remind you of somebody you know personally. These people create their own bad karma.

Sometimes people don't get the karmic lesson the first time, so they create a situation for learning it again. Some of these individuals just keep doing the same dance and calling it *bad luck*. It can be unsettling to take ownership of what occurs in our life. It can be difficult at times for anyone to admit wrongdoing. We all make mistakes. We have all had to repeat the same lesson every now and then in our life. It is not about blame. It is simply about our own spiritual development.

To give you ideas of specific times when individuals may attract negative karma, a list is provided here.

Things That May Attract Negative Karma:

1) Ethical dilemmas

2) Integrity issues

3) Stealing

4) Infidelity

5) Physically, mentally, or emotionally harming another living thing

Alternatively, there are times when we carry out certain actions that result in attracting positive karma. A list of some of those times is listed here.

Things That May Attract Good Karma:

1) Treating others with kindness

2) Doing good deeds for others

3) Charity

4) Honesty

5) Being ethical even when it is a tough decision

6) Spreading love to other living things—physically, mentally, or emotionally

If you see a pattern in your life and want to change it, get the karmic lesson behind the event as soon as you can—and move on.

9~Teaching Others How to Treat You

Karma gives you and others the spiritual lessons needed to move forward. Their lessons are theirs; yours are personal to you. Acknowledging the existence of karma doesn't mean that you should abandon taking responsibility for yourself when others step on your toes. Being responsible means that if you don't like the way you're being treated, it's your duty to change it. If somebody is taking advantage of you, don't allow it. If somebody is asking you to do things you don't want to do, say no. Remember, others learn to treat you as you *teach* them to treat you.

How do you teach others to treat you the way that you want to be treated? You do this by setting boundaries, identifying what you decide is and isn't acceptable. Boundaries vary from person to person. For example, although I consider myself a giving person, what I would deem acceptable for family and close friends may not be acceptable for an acquaintance. Close friends and family members know that they can call on me at any time, day or night. However, I would prefer an acquaintance to contact me at a reasonable time during the day. It takes self-esteem to set boundaries with someone. In effect, you're saying, "I am worthy of this kind of treatment, and anything less is unacceptable."

You'll notice that people will "get" your boundaries, even without your having to state them aloud. Your demeanor itself influences the message you send. People know who they can or cannot take advantage of, even if they don't consciously acknowledge their intentions.

Other examples of boundaries are:

1) I discourage incessant cursing around me or at me and will say so.

2) I expect honesty and integrity in all of my relationships.

3) I expect to be treated with respect.

4) I expect people to call before they stop by my home.

5) I appreciate relationships that allow me to give and receive; they are not one-sided.

Much of how others treat you is subconscious; they learn certain behaviors just like a dog learns to beg for a treat. Perhaps you've sent mixed messages without even realizing it. If that is the case, set the intention that being treated a particular way will no longer be acceptable to you. Then once you say it, stand by it. At times you may have to state the new boundary, but often individuals will just pick up on the change within you.

When you set boundaries, also be prepared for the consequences. Some people may not be willing to live by your new terms, but that is okay. One person leaving makes room for somebody else to fill that space. Most likely, the person filling the opening will be a better fit with the boundaries you currently have set.

10~Aligning with Your Soul's Purpose

Whether you call it your purpose, path, or calling doesn't matter—as long as you acknowledge it and live it! Your path is your soul's purpose for being born. It is my belief that this was determined prior to your birth as an agreement between you and your Creator. You have unique talents and gifts that will assist you with carrying out your purpose. It doesn't matter specifically who you believe your Creator to be or what religion you align most closely with. The point is that these unique talents and gifts that make you different from anybody else are your tools to carry out your mission, which is specific to you.

Regardless of the belief system that you have, you were born with a calling when you arrived on earth. Now it's up to you to go inward, remember it, and live it out. Along the way, free will is available to you, and you can be detoured away from your purpose. Free will allows you to make choices. The decisions that you make will determine how you will get to your destination. Sometimes the decisions you make through free will aren't necessarily dedicated to your highest good, taking you on the aforementioned detour. Sometimes fate steps in when you veer off the path. Fate leads you to opportunities, places, people, and things that you are meant to encounter even without your doing anything to bring about events.

Some find their groove and seemingly live their plan almost from the beginning. Others take time to find their purpose. It's possible to get pulled off course when you stop tuning in to your internal radar and give more validity to what others say instead of what you know to be right for you. Remember, in most cases when you are tuned in, nobody knows what's best for you better than you do. Think of all of the distorted ideas people have about their purpose. This often results from others trying to *help* them figure it out. Sadly, most of the distortion happens when you don't take time to reflect on the information that you already have. Consider the source prior to giving validity to what anyone says. Often those who derail others from their direct routes are overbooked, busy being busy, and perpetually focused on fixing somebody else's life. Subconsciously, they're avoiding what needs to be fixed in their own lives. Is that the source of the advice you want to take?

Look at what you were drawn to as a child, knowing you came in already on your path. What did you enjoy playing most? What did you want to be and why? What would you do if you didn't need to earn a living? Let answers to these questions guide your actions.

When I was little, I loved to play nurse. When asked why I wanted to be a nurse, I said "So I can help people." When I was growing up I did not have any knowledge of complementary modalities. Today, nursing isn't my chosen profession, but I always knew I wanted to help people. That purpose can be carried out in many career fields. We are not born to carry out a certain job title or career, but to carry out our purpose in the way that feels most natural to us.

In a similar way, look at your gifts and desires. What kinds of jobs allow you to do what you like and what you're good at? What type of career would be ideal for you? Examining your natural skills and abilities will further assist you in uncovering your path. Are you gifted with musical, artistic, or athletic talents? Do you find that your expertise lies in understanding and relating to people and their needs? Do you have a knack for fixing things? Have you always had a special bond with animals? You'll find the answers inside. Those who are highly successful—in any meaning of the word—learned to believe in their path and follow their dreams. When you're doing what's meant for you, you can excel naturally.

It makes sense to presume that once you're fulfilling your soul's purpose, your life will flow more smoothly. At the same time, remember that your job or career doesn't define who you are as a person. For the most part, it takes up a large percentage of your time, thus awarding you the greatest opportunity in which to feel fulfilled if you choose a career that is aligned with your purpose. If you're not making your mark on the world through your career, you can fulfill your purpose through charity work or by simply being the person you are guided to be.

It all comes together by seeing your calling not as either/or but as part of a whole. I know I'm not only supposed to help others through coaching, energy work, or hypnosis; I'm also drawn to fulfill my purpose through charities such as local animal rescues, local church groups, or just by helping others who are truly in need. Every day, I strive to fulfill my purpose in every aspect of my life. When you uncover your soul's purpose and are able to integrate it into your life, you'll positively affect the way you feel about your life. It will give you a heightened sense of satisfaction in all that you do.

Participate in the short exercise that follows to determine what drives you, to help you uncover what your soul's purpose might be.

Example:

Recommendation: Close your eyes, and use your imagination after reading each of the following questions to help you to envision your answers. Notice what you see, feel, and hear as you consider each question.

1) When you picture your life one year from now, what are you doing? Why are you doing it?

   Running my own business- It is what I have always dreamed of doing.

2) When you picture your life five years from now, what are you doing? Why are you doing it?

   Still running my own business but with multiple locations. I am fulfilling my dreams.

3) Are you enjoying the legacy you want to leave behind? What do you want to be known for? How can you fulfill that legacy?

Yes, I am known for helping others with the wealth that I created from running my business.

4) What drives you? What are you passionate about?

Helping others

5) What creates the most emotion within you, negative or positive? Why?

It fills my heart to make other people happy. When I see them smile as a result of my actions, it makes me happy too.

Recommendation: Close your eyes, and use your imagination after reading each of the following questions to help you to envision your answers. Notice what you see, feel, and hear as you consider each question.

1) When you picture your life one year from now, what are you doing? Why are you doing it?

_____

_____

2) When you picture your life five years from now, what are you doing? Why are you doing it?

_____

_____

3) Are you enjoying the legacy you want to leave behind? What do you want to be known for? How can you fulfill that legacy?

_____

_____

4) What drives you? What are you passionate about?

   _____

   _____

5) What creates the most emotion within
   you, negative or positive? Why?

   _____

   _____

When you uncover that which you are truly passionate about, you will begin to uncover that which
drives you. Your life purpose is the drive within
you and will elicit emotions, even when you have
yet to uncover what your purpose is. As you begin
to uncover the answers to the questions, you will
see a pattern, an underlying pull that was always
there, driving you to do what you were meant to do.

11~Plotting Your Journey and Tuning in to Your GPS

When you truly realize what you're meant to do and set your boundaries for how you will achieve that, you'll begin to feel more freedom! You identify what you can and can't do. You get to decide when enough is enough. You get to set the limits—or no limits at all.

You have gone through a number of exercises designed to help you uncover your desires, align with your soul's purpose, and more. As you continue to grow, your desires, needs, and even your dreams will evolve. Being in touch with what you desire, learning who you are, and being open to guidance from your intuition to assist you in getting there will help you to build the life you aspire to create.

When you were a child and daydreamed about what you'd be when you grew up, chances are you saw no limitations. Today, think back to what you used to dream of; recall what you wanted to be. Where did you want to live? How did you want to live?

Unfortunately, as people get older, they forget their earliest daydreams and desires. But those who choose a path of enlightenment will spend countless hours uncovering and deciphering the early daydreams they trusted as children.

Depending on how much or how little others encouraged you to be yourself growing up, you may or may not have realized that you are never completely alone in making a decision. Many choices in life are actually made, in part, with the help of messages from your spirit, such as through a nudge or inner voice reassuring you to go the way that feels right to you. Yes, you have an internal radar helping you choose your mate, select a career, find a place to live, pick a car to drive, and even decide on a pet to adopt. It also helps you know when and if it's time to have children, and even guides adoptive parents to those they are meant to adopt.

Follow that which you know you are passionate about, and be open to guidance from your internal radar to get there. If you are not sure what that is, perhaps you haven't found it yet. It will present itself at the perfect time. Your passion is that thing that drives you, burns within your belly, and leads you to success in whatever you do. This combines your soul's purpose with all the fine details to make your life the life that was meant for you.

Once you learn how to listen to this internal radar, it will prove to be one of the best decision-making resources in your life. It will feel like those good ol' days of carefree daydreaming! This tool, once fine-tuned, will prove to be effective in plotting your journey as well as carrying out the tasks of your everyday life.

I learned to rely on my inner GPS quite early for some areas of my life. During my college years, I worked as the manager of a retail store and would rely on my inner radar to help me to choose who would or would not be a good hire. I only had to disregard this inner radar once to learn that doing so could end up being a bad decision for me.

Applicants could say all of the right things, but somehow I would just get a feeling that they were not the right fit, despite what they were saying. On the occasion that I disregarded what my inner guidance was telling me, the potential hire was so good at interviewing that I thought my inner guidance had to be mistaken in thinking the individual in question would not be a terrific employee. However, once hired, the individual showed up late, took long breaks, had a poor work ethic, and ultimately had to be terminated within thirty days of her start date.

I continued to rely on my inner guidance when making hiring decisions, using it to determine who I would surround myself with. In another job, my supervisor would get impatient with me because I'd allow my *gut* to decide which person to hire or not hire rather quickly. I'd have made my decision within the first five minutes of an interview, while she'd go through painful hours of rehearsed questions. After a while, I'd close up my folder as a sign I wasn't willing to waste any more time with the applicant. She couldn't understand why I would have my mind made up so quickly in the interview. Without exception, whenever she'd override my gut feeling and hire someone against my better judgment, it turned out to be a poor choice.

I came to rely on my internal GPS to help me find the right house when my husband and I were shopping for a new home. If you have ever shopped for a home, you know that you *just know* when you are in the home that was meant for you. You also know that it is not always about the home being the biggest or best on the block as much as how it *feels right,* sometimes for reasons you can't even describe. That feeling is your internal GPS letting you know you have found the place where you are meant to live. My husband and I were shown several homes during our search before we stepped into the home we eventually purchased. We saw many houses that would have been suitable for us, but for one reason or another they just didn't feel right to me—much to my husband's frustration at times. When we were finally shown the home that we purchased, I knew from the moment I stepped in the front door that it was where we were meant to live. We purchased the home and couldn't be happier with our decision. It turned out to be the right home in the right area with the right neighbors for us.

What if there are times when we may not listen to what our internal radar is telling us? Learn from them and move on! Become more acquainted with what it feels like when you are being given guidance. Stand in your power, learning your lessons. We all have our own. Reflect on times that you did follow your internal GPS. As you become more in touch with using the guidance system we are all equipped with, remember that all of your life experiences have culminated to make you who you are meant to be in that moment. Take the positive and leave the rest where it belongs—in the past. Learn to rely on what you know to be right for you, regardless of what others say. Practice with little decisions that are less pertinent when you are first getting used to what it feels like. Have patience with yourself as you learn to use your internal radar. It's like mastering a complicated technological device. Some will understand it quickly, and others will take time to get used to it. You are all learning on precisely the right schedule for you.

Remember, when you reconnect with who you truly are, you will find that you have always had aspirations of what you wanted to do in terms of a career; who you formed relationships with; where, how, and with whom you wanted to live; and what you were meant to accomplish. We are all born with our own guidance systems. Allowing your internal guidance system to usher you through life can prove to be a valuable resource leading you to what you desire. Once connected, you will be able to plot a journey that awakens your passions.

12~Creating Peace amid Chaos

When you go through the process I described in the previous chapters and get reacquainted with who you are, it becomes easier to handle whatever comes your way.

You begin to feel more like yourself and can feel a connection to your Creator. You feel closer to your source: spirit. How do you know you are moving closer to spirit? You start to see how synchronicities work. You notice that when one thing is taken away, another is presented.

The secret is to always expect good things to come, even when a situation may be unpleasant. When you're looking for good things, you'll be open to seeing them. As a result, you'll be better equipped to take advantage of opportunities that arise. When things or individuals that are not suited for you leave, don't try to hold onto them. You're cutting deadwood out of your life.

Often we mourn the loss of certain things—not because we wanted them, but because we didn't control their departure or perhaps our egos got wrapped up in whatever we lost. Some people mourn breakups or the loss of a job when, in fact, it was the universe's or your Higher Power's way of making room for something better to come along.

Sometimes your life begins to evolve even if you haven't taken steps yet to change anything. Individuals have often had epiphanies that they need to eradicate something from their lives and in the next moment discovered that it has already been eliminated. It is possible for your intention to be so strong that it starts a domino effect. When you step back and acknowledge that certain situations aren't a good fit for you, you can begin clearing them from your life. At that point, you're open to something that's a better fit. By making this decision, you begin to set the intention that you are ready for change in that area of your life. Just because you didn't actively set the changes in motion, it doesn't mean your intentions didn't!

So often we complain about something we want to change in our lives. Yet when it's taken away, we dwell on it, asking why—only to miss a better opportunity that came along. We'd been too busy concentrating on how wronged we felt.

When you realize you aren't in chaos but in complete control of your life, you get to make decisions based on what does or doesn't fit in your life anymore. You get to decide what's right for you and what direction you want to go. If you feel like you haven't been able to find your navigating ability yet, that's okay. Be gentle with yourself. You haven't learned to listen to your spirit yet. Spirit always knows what you *need*. In contrast, ego decides what you *want*.

Remember, your spirit knows why you're here, what you're meant to do, and how you're meant to use your abilities to accomplish your purpose. That information can assist you in maneuvering any storm that you are faced with.

When you're tuned in to your spirit, it doesn't mean you never have disappointments again. You will experience fewer disappointments as your life flows more easily. You'll put up less resistance and take fewer detours than you did in the past to get to your destination.

You have the choice amid confusing times to either hold onto your power or give in to the chaos around you, offering your power up to the chaos instead. Trust that every moment of every day you're exactly where you are meant to be, experiencing exactly what you are meant to experience.

Does this all sound great but you need proof? Perfect! Look at your life. Recall every pivotal moment in your life—especially the tough ones. These are some of the moments that had the greatest impact on molding you into who you are today. During each incident, you may nearly have been knocked to your knees with emotion. Some moments may have felt downright surreal. Although there is no denying the turmoil that you felt at the time, did each of these incidents shape you in a positive manner? Did each of these moments in time serve to give you a nugget or tool that you still deem valuable today? Now imagine being able to go through those same moments knowing that you would be all right and would even get something positive from each and every one of them. You just created your own argument to bring yourself back to peace in chaos. Of course you will be all right. You will even get something positive out of it in the end. Do what you need to do, and realize there is no sense in focusing on anything but the positive in each moment that you experience.

Disappointments are part of life, but you get to *choose* how they'll affect you. It's not about having a perfect life but about getting back to your natural state of being—a state of peace— by trusting that everything has its place. You do this by having confidence that nothing is permanent, neither the good nor the bad, and knowing that if something doesn't feel good, it will pass.

13~Making the Right Choices for You

If you are still having trouble determining which guidance is from your internal radar and which is from your ego, remember that the right choice for you is the one dedicated to your highest good. A decision that serves your highest good doesn't harm you or anyone else. Rather, it's best for all involved. If a choice you make causes pain to others, it probably isn't dedicated to your highest good; it might just be what you think you want. You might not be tuning in to your spirit at all. So take a step back and reflect. Your ego might be getting the best of you.

Here are signs that a decision was driven by the ego:

1) Stealing

2) Lying to get what you want

3) Feeling guilty: "But it's what I have to do"

4) Feeling bad: "But it's what works best for me"

5) Cheating on anything for any reason

6) Partaking in any action that would be considered unethical: "But I have to" or "It's what everybody is doing"

7) Considering only yourself and your own happiness in making the decision

In contrast, here are signs that a decision was driven by your spirit:

1) "It just feels right"

2) "I am ready to be of service to others"

3) "Everything just fell into place"

4) "It's like that was made for me"

5) The situation allows you to abide by all of your morals

6) The decision honors all parties involved

7) The decision would be considered ethical even if it feels difficult because somebody else isn't getting what *they* want

Despite the fact that some decisions can be challenging to make at times, remember that you are equipped with a connection to spirit that can assist you in making the right decision for yourself at any time. You can tell if a decision is "right" or aligns with your spirit by how it "feels" to you or by the verbiage you use when you describe it. Regardless of how connected you are to your spirit, it is giving you clues in everything you do. So when in doubt, stop, listen, and feel what and how you are feeling and listen to what you are saying about the questions you are faced with.

14~Detaching from the Outcome

Do you allow things to happen on their own, or do you press for a certain outcome? Deciding that something needs to happen right away—and being attached to a specific outcome—can create obstacles in your life. Concerning yourself solely with that outcome is self-limiting, and forcing things into a particular time frame inhibits flow.

Instead, open yourself to seeing the truth as it comes to you in perfect time. When you sit back and let things happen, everything unfolds. That's when you'll make way for miracles. It's easy to miss what's in front of you if you get hung up on looking at what *isn't* an option anymore or isn't happening fast enough. Keep in mind that even when you're divinely guided, you won't always get all the directions at once.

When life doesn't work out as planned, it's important to keep your mind positive. That will make the difference between creating a whole new world and perpetuating the old one. You must have the right mindset to acknowledge solutions, opportunities, and even the right people when they walk into your life to make it the one you desire. Then, when things fall into place, you'll feel encouraged that events are turning around for the better. Every improvement that you show gratitude for will help to create new and bigger changes in your life.

Here's an example from my life. When I was still working in corporate America, my supervisor and his supervisor set up a phone conference with me. My direct manager was being promoted, and they informed me that they wanted me to take on his role. I was flattered and truly elated to have been not only thought of, but handpicked for his position. As a technicality, I needed to go through the interview process, but the two led me to believe that for all intents and purposes, the job was mine. My supervisor needed to step into his new role as soon as possible, so as always I rose to the occasion and covered for him, handling anything that fell under his job description while still carrying out my own job. I continued to happily cover the duties of both my supervisor's and my own position for more than eight months.

Much to my dismay, when my supervisor's replacement was announced, it turned out to be somebody from another department. I had been passed over. In the previous eight months, I had done such an excellent job doing the work of two people that the region I was supervising received an award for the first time in its existence. This award was not presented to me but to the replacement, who had only just been given the title. Although I was hurt, I knew I had to make the best of it or move on. I showed my new supervisor that she could trust me. I even ended up training her. My new supervisor appreciated my loyalty so much that I was given a $60,000 raise the first year that I reported to her.

The fact that I was passed over woke me up and motivated me to stop allowing the company I worked for to dominate my life. I was working more than sixty hours per week, was available seven days per week, was always the go-to person for employees even if they didn't report to me, and was giving the company far too much of my life. I began to pursue interests outside of work and instill balance in my life. I gave my 100 percent to the job when I was there, but I saw that I would be just as effective if I took "me" time as well.

This is what inspired me to take classes and find my true passion in the holistic community. If I had been given the promotion as promised, I probably never would have slowed down and thought about my own needs. Because of the disappointment, I realized the importance of balance in my life. I continued to study for years while keeping my job, allowing me to find my passion and fine-tune the tools that I learned. As I was able to enjoy my life more when it was brought into balance, I appreciated the company as well as the people I worked with more. Today, my new supervisor remains a dear friend. The results far surpassed whatever I thought was meant for me. I am grateful that I was able to concentrate on my desire to succeed in life rather than on what I thought I wanted: to be promoted. Clearly, everything happened just as it was meant to.

To curb your impatience, break things down into little celebrations. Acknowledge *everything* that you manifest along the way, big or small. Be grateful. Focus on the good that you pull in. Say "yes" to things that align with the new life you're creating. Look for signs that indicate you're closer to what you've dreamed of, like seeing what you desire all around you and in acquaintances that you meet. Get excited when you see how far you've come and what you can create—simply by changing your thoughts.

How long does it take to make the changes we desire? As long as needed. Sometimes it's a question of divine timing, changing our beliefs, or seeing through our blind spots. We have all had our own hurdles to jump. These hurdles are often our own *truths* that become our obstacles to moving forward: "It takes money to make money." "The good guy always finishes last." "If you want to get ahead, you have to put in your time." Don't confuse your truth with what is considered universally true. Be willing to challenge your own beliefs. Yes, it will take money for you to make money, if that is what you believe to be true. Yes, the good guy will always finish last if that is what you expect. Yes, it *has* to take time if that's what you believe.

Learn to distinguish the difference between your belief system acting as an obstacle and the situation just being a case of *divine timing*. You know in your heart if you have always had expectations of "needing to put in your time" to earn anything you want in life. You also can distinguish when you have done everything you were guided to do, while all signs point to your being on the right path but, you still feel like you are in a holding pattern. It is important to be honest with yourself about whether or not you have done what you were guided to do to move forward. Acknowledging this will help you to determine your role in moving forward.

What does divine timing mean? It could mean that other individuals need to prepare for or be a part of what you are attempting to achieve. It can be a case of the timing needing to be right so individuals are who they will become at the time you achieve your desire, or maybe others need to shift their perspectives to be more accepting of what you will offer. Do you get the idea?

Most of all, understand that you can't set the timing for change. Trust the divine clock, and celebrate the journey along the way. When you stop waiting for a certain outcome, you will look at life differently, knowing it will be different with each day; you'll pay attention. You'll notice new things you might not have seen before—like the beauty of a sunrise when you wake up early in the morning and how it makes the rich taste of a freshly brewed cup of coffee taste better. In this frame of mind, a smile will tickle you a little bit more; it will matter less if somebody wants to pull in front of you when you are driving. At the end of the day, you'll start to see meaning in all that you do, and you won't depend on specific outcomes for your sense of joy. When you do achieve what your spirit is guiding you to, it will be everything you have ever wanted and more. In your new more positive state of mind, you will be even more fulfilled than you can imagine.

15~What if We Have Refused to Hear What Our Spirit is Yelling at Us?

Things happen, but if you're getting the same message over and over, the next time you sit in meditation ask for help understanding what lesson you're missing. Sometimes when things happen—especially when they are repeated—a lesson is ripe to be learned. At times, you refuse to hear the lesson that is being offered, and it gets louder as the opportunities to discover what you may not be hearing continue to present themselves. Just because a lesson awaits, that doesn't mean you deserved whatever occurred. Referring back to the patterns that you develop in your life can sometimes lead you to a message you may be overlooking.

From time to time, these lessons may result from our not listening to our guidance to begin with. We have all made decisions that, despite our feeling apprehensive, we went ahead with, and then we refused to change direction once our course was set. That feeling of "apprehension" is our spirit speaking to us. Whether it is a relationship that we are not sure about, a career, a house, a move, a car, or something else, we cannot make a decision fit just by sticking with it if it is not right for us.

Our soul may be longing to work in a career that fulfills our life's purpose. As we continue to silence our internal radar, an unprecedented number of individuals remain unemployed. People go through the motions of applying for jobs that are carbon copies of the ones they were laid off from, never stopping to recognize that they may never have liked the job in the first place. Some individuals do this to chase large incomes; for others it is just familiar. Does this sound like you? Do you or somebody you know continue to search for a career in a field that you have spent years complaining about? Is your spirit guiding you to something new, but you just won't listen? Have you made every excuse to not pursue that which you are most passionate about, including excuses of affordability, time, and anything else you could think of while just wasting more time and continuing to stay unemployed? When individuals tune in to their true callings, they open the doors to abundance.

Don't hide from what was meant to be your life's purpose! Don't stay in a situation that causes you to feel *stuck* in any way. Don't turn off positive guidance that you are being given repeatedly. This may be for your highest good. You're doing yourself a disservice if you don't stop and consider your options. You're meant to be in the exact situation you are in, going through exactly what you are going through, so you can apply the knowledge gained later in your life.

When you are not listening, the lesson gets more difficult. Some lessons are harder to get than others, but if you are open to it, eventually you will get the message and be able to apply it to whatever obstacles you are currently facing. Certainly you have patterns in your life that represent lessons you haven't yet recognized.

We get stubborn and do the same thing over and over expecting different results. We get more persistent but refuse to change directions regardless of what the signs are telling us. Despite our rational side, we have all done this at one time or another. We dig our heels into the ground, determined to make something work that hasn't, although from the beginning we have seen red flags. We may even try changing our execution plan, determined to make it work this time. We put our blood, sweat, and tears into it. We are determined to force it to work, even though if we were to slow down and think about it, we really wouldn't want it in the first place. No wonder we feel like we have things coming at us from every direction at times like that; those are messages screaming for us to change direction.

We discussed the existence of divine timing. There is a difference between guidance screaming for you to change directions and divine timing. Learn to distinguish them. Is it a case of timing, or are you ignoring messages that you are being given? When it seems like nothing is working, take time to see if you are missing something. Look at your life, and evaluate if you're acting in accordance with your highest good. One distinguishing characteristic telling you that you may be overlooking a message that is being repeated to you is that you may feel like you are being nudged to do something, but you are just not getting it. You may feel restless or even uneasy but not know why. Stop, meditate, and tune in for guidance on what this all means.

Lessons can be hard to learn, but they are worth it. When you stay focused and see the positive in the moment, even when it feels like everything is falling apart around you, you'll be led to something better suited for you; expect something positive. Life can be tough and amazing. It can be both at the same time.

You can turn your life around any time that YOU choose. You really can have storms all around you and still choose to see the positive. A portion of the positive is the guidance you are receiving with a solution to the dilemma you are facing. As you begin to go within and follow your guidance, you will notice peace being restored around you. With each little shift, you will receive more proof that your life is turning a corner. When you decide it is time for a change, work on *yourself* first, and then watch the world change around you. It's an amazing sight to see. Be willing to be vulnerable in this process. Seek professional help if it is needed. Be kind to yourself and acknowledge you are just human, and commend yourself for doing the work to find your peace.

New opportunities will present themselves. You may notice options that have always been available to you that you have never paid attention to. The key is to realize there is a reason for everything. It's up to you to go within to figure it out.

16~Making a Decision to Love Yourself

Starting today, make a decision to love yourself. Some of you might not know where to begin or you might think the idea sounds foreign. Some of you might be in denial, thinking you already love yourself while your actions prove otherwise. Others may love the idea but are in need of guidance. Some of you may truly love yourselves. How do you sift through your internal dialogue to really know how you feel? If you find yourself *loving* who you are but then indulge in self-deprecating acts, watch out. You could be sabotaging yourself as if you were your own worst enemy.

It's easy to be kind to your family and friends, but difficult to extend yourself that same degree of kindness. Do you treat yourself as well as you treat everyone else? Some individuals say things about themselves they would never say about their friends, family, or even somebody they don't like. Watch your internal dialogue. One client, whom I will call James, continuously called himself "dumb." When I asked why he would use that term to describe himself, he said he was only joking. Pressing a little further, I asked if he would joke that way about others. He realized that he had a habit of calling himself dumb all day long. If asked, James would have said he loved himself, yet he continued to speak unkind words when describing his intellect.

When you decide to love yourself, you act in accordance with your highest good. You speak and think about yourself as you would a dear friend. You see the best in yourself while acknowledging the flaws that make you human. Denying them won't pave the way to self-enlightenment, but accepting them will.

When I was in management, I was responsible for employee evaluations. The livelihood of each employee that I worked with was affected by what I said. I wanted my appraisals to be done without bias, and to do this I needed to like each of them. I considered it important to make an effort to get to know every employee personally. I would ask them about themselves and find out their hot buttons, what made them tick, what their family dynamics were like, and anything else they were willing to share. I would just keep digging until I could find a nugget to hold onto that would allow me to see the *good* that was in each of them. This *good* that I was digging for was their soul, or who they truly were without their public façades. Sometimes I felt like I was on a treasure hunt. Some individuals hid their true selves deep inside.

As I continued to go through this process with each new report, it always confirmed that each person was beautiful on the inside when I took the time to get to know them. Regardless of how hidden each soul was, I found there was something exquisite in everyone just waiting to come out. Going through what was sometimes a lengthy process with these individuals reminded me that it was important to do this for myself in times of insecurities too. I had to take pause and realize that if in my busy schedule I made time to do this with everyone else, it was equally important to remember to do it for myself, as well. The same is true for you, so if you don't love yourself, get digging and find your inner beauty!

Answer the following questions to uncover the beauty that lies within you. When answering each question, remember to be your own biggest fan. Be as kind to yourself as you would be to a dear friend. Allow yourself to see and understand what makes you tick. Knowing who you are and what makes you tick will help you in the process of loving yourself.

Example:

What Makes You Tick?

1) What do you like to do?

Yoga and going to the gym

2) What do you absolutely love?

Traveling and reading

3) What's interesting about you?

I lived in 10 states in the first 17 years of my life.

4) What makes you unique?

I love to be the center of attention, but I am also sensitive to the person who is too shy to join in.

5) What role do you play in your family?

I am the peacemaker.

6) What makes you laugh?

I love witty humor. I like comedians who are so funny that they don't have to be dirty to be funny.

7) What is impressive about you?

If I set my mind on something, I will accomplish it.

8) What are your greatest accomplishments?

Purchasing my condo and getting my master's degree

9) What dreams do you have for your future?

Traveling to Australia and New Zealand and making a difference in the world

What Makes You Tick?

1) What do you like to do?

_____

_____

_____

2) What do you absolutely love?

_____

_____

_____

3) What's interesting about you?

_____

_____

_____

4) What makes you unique?

_____

_____

_____

5) What role do you play in your family?

_____

_____

_____

6) What makes you laugh?

_____

_____

_____

7) What is impressive about you?

_____

_____

_____

8) What are your greatest accomplishments?

_____

_____

_____

9) What dreams do you have for your future?

_____

_____

_____

After you answer each question about yourself, take time to read your responses. Remember your triumphs, appreciate what makes you shine, and look forward to the dreams you have for the future that are unique to you. If doubts or insecurities arise, pull your responses out and remind yourself of who you truly are.

17~Taking Care of Your Vessel

An integral part of the mind-body-spirit connection is your body—the vehicle for the mind and the spirit. Just as you can't expect your car to run smoothly with poor maintenance, you can't expect your body to do so. Exercise daily. Pay attention to what you fuel your body with. Nourish it with healthy food and a balanced diet. Listen to what your aches and pains are telling you.

How you treat your body is a direct reflection of how you feel about yourself. Look around, and you will see that the number of overweight Americans is growing—literally. Obesity is one of the leading causes of disease, but our nation just continues to grow. On the other side of the scale, some people continue to cut calories so much that they are not giving their bodies the nourishment they need.

Being obese or underweight is not a question of vanity. They are both health concerns. If you have been told by your doctor to make healthy changes to your weight, follow his or her recommendations.

Remember, having a healthy body affects your mind and spirit in a positive way, while having an unhealthy body impacts your mind and spirit in a negative way. It doesn't matter what was affected first. Nourish them all, and they will support one another.

Most people know how to eat properly, and if they don't, it's not due to lack of information. Today, more than ever, we can access helpful resources by visiting a library, asking a doctor, seeing a nutritionist or dietician, or searching online. It's shocking the number of people who just don't make it a priority to pay attention to what they're taking in. Many of the diseases that we suffer from can be avoided or alleviated by simply changing our diet. Moderation is key. Too much of anything is not good, but we can also deprive our bodies of essential vitamins and nutrients if we are not eating a balanced diet.

Unlike many crazes in our society, being healthy is a lifestyle choice, not a fleeting fad. So take responsibility for what you put into your body. Educating yourself about what's healthy or not helps you hedge temptations to splurge that come your way. Would you be less likely to give into cravings for unhealthy food if you fully understood the ramifications on your body when you make unhealthy choices? Seek experts who can help you. By arming yourself with information about health, you can explore nutritious alternatives to unhealthy habits that you might have.

There really is truth to the old cliché "garbage in, garbage out." Become your own advocate. Read labels when you are shopping and learn what they really mean. One hot topic is the use of GMOs (genetically modified organisms). There has been discussion about health concerns related to GMOs and whether or not labels should be required for GMO foods. Being informed will allow you to make better choices for your nutritional needs.

If you want to be more productive, have more energy, think more clearly, sleep better, and experience countless other positive benefits—start exercising. Talk to your doctor about the right type of exercise for you, and inquire if you are healthy enough to begin an exercise routine. Regardless of how hectic your schedule is, this is essential. Find time. Fit it in. You need it. If you're busy with children, make them part of your exercise routine. Children need to start learning from a young age that exercise is an integral part of living a healthy lifestyle. It is important to show this to your children. If you aren't sure where to start or if you aren't sure if your child is healthy enough to exercise, have a discussion with your pediatrician. You and your child will both receive body-mind-spirit advantages, and everyone involved will look forward to this special bonding time. Once you get started, you will be amazed by the benefits.

The more in tune you become with your body, the more you will recognize when an imbalance is occurring. Physical aches and pains can affect the mind and spirit. Unresolved emotional or spiritual pain can cause physical pain. It doesn't matter what comes first. The point is that you are a whole person, not separate from any portion of yourself.

Your body is a magnificent instrument. There is a reason for everything that you experience—even sensations in your body. Unlike a car, you do not come equipped with dashboard lights to let you know what your body needs. You do have emotions, aches, and pains to tell you when there are imbalances, though. If you ignore the emotional pain, your body will eventually use physical pain to get your attention and vice versa. Sometimes our emotions take the form of a nagging ache that is nothing more than that—an annoying ache. Other times, our emotions take form as disease in our bodies. Sometimes they lie somewhere in between. It is important to not only seek medical attention for these symptoms, but also to meditate on them and ask what those symptoms are telling you.

I experienced very real knee pain—a torn medial meniscus—that required surgery to repair. The injury occurred when I was preparing to graduate from high school, and it became aggravated when I was preparing to graduate from college. After meditating on the pain and its meaning, I realized I was apprehensive about graduating and moving on to the next phase of my life. My knee was repaired through surgery, but my doctor informed me that I would eventually get arthritis due to the injury. Finding this prognosis to be unacceptable, I took measures to strengthen and support my knee. Today, twenty years later, I continue to move forward confidently in life—in all areas, especially athletically—enjoying long-distance running, arthritis free. What helped me? Was it my knee being repaired? Was moving forward with my life what helped my knee? The answer is that it doesn't matter. They both supported each other. When I worked on one area, the other benefited too. If you are not sure what a symptom in your body is telling you, meditate on it, and be open to the insight you receive.

Do what you can to maintain a healthy body. Evaluate what you are doing to your precious vessel—your body. Are you taking care of it? Are you making its care a priority? Yes, life is busy, but at the end of the day, you need your body *healthy* to accomplish all of that busyness.

18~Being Kind to Your Spirit

It's guaranteed that you'll do what you consider *messing up* sometimes. You are human and, despite having good intentions, you'll slip. Traffic may still annoy you some days, unkind people may still make you angry occasionally, others may still hurt your feelings, you will make decisions you wish you hadn't, and sometimes you just might not feel like yourself. When this happens, be kind to yourself. At the same time, accept when you're doing wrong, apologize for it if need be, and move on. Obsessing over something you did *wrong* doesn't fix it; staying in a holding pattern of regret keeps you stuck.

The more you become comfortable with accepting the message and moving on, the more you will realize there really are no mistakes—just lessons you are ready to learn. That is all just part of your human experience! Be okay with making mistakes because you'll learn from them. Have the confidence to change directions if that's best for you. Always remember there's a divine purpose for everything in your life. When you trust that everything has a purpose—even if you don't see it at the moment— you develop the muscle within you that's able to see the positivity in everything, and that is when your life will change for the better.

It's normal to have moments that aren't our best. We are only human. It's easy to get hung up on needing to be perfect and forgetting that even teachers need lessons to grow. No one has all of the answers. When we allow our lessons to negatively impact our reflection, this disconnects us from spirit. We are all here to learn our own lessons on our own paths. When we can be forgiving with ourselves and others, life will flow much more smoothly.

Even though you're working toward enlightenment, your flaws will still show up. Don't be disheartened; they exist for a reason, even when you don't see or acknowledge them. They make you human. If you find that you receive a message repeatedly within your life, when the theme comes to the surface, embrace it and be open to what each situation is trying to tell you. It may be your spirit's way of letting you know it is time to overcome a new hurdle in your life. Jin Shin Jyutsu® —an ancient Japanese art of harmonizing energy—taught me that the things I consider distasteful in others are what I wish not to see in myself. It taught me to step back when I find something distasteful about somebody else and ask myself what to work on in myself. It has made me more patient with others. When you get these messages, as they arise, keep in mind that you are human, too!

How you react and the compassion you are able to show when you view yourself as less than perfect will determine whether or not you allow yourself to stay connected to spirit during the times when you are most in need. Being unkind to yourself creates a disconnect between yourself and your spirit. It causes you to feel separation from the one who can prove to be your greatest resource in times of need. When you were going through a particularly difficult time in your life, you may remember feeling completely alone even though you were in a room full of people,. You may also remember that throughout some of the toughest times, you were able to stay positive, and you felt surrounded by love, even when you were alone. The difference in each situation is the strength of your connection to spirit.

Think back to an event when you were truly happy—a moment that represents complete bliss to you. It may be when you accomplished a special goal, your wedding day, the birth of your child, or something else entirely. It doesn't matter what caused your happiness. It just matters that you experienced it. True happiness lights you up from the inside. It is as if there is a beam of light coming from within, shining out of each pore of your body. That is your spirit's way of glowing from within. That is what it feels like when you are truly connected.

Now recall a time when you felt disappointment so deeply that it not only affected your emotions but also weakened your body and your will—your spirit. You may recall feeling alone or disconnected at that time. What you were doing is preventing yourself from feeling your connection to spirit. Some of us do this a little bit every day with our thoughts or the treatment we give ourselves when we focus on when stumbled rather than when we soared. It may not feel as impactful as those events you just reflected upon, but over time this can cause a lasting impression.

Being kind to your spirit means acknowledging the divine within you and being patient with your imperfections along the way. That means you understand that we are all here to learn and that nobody is perfect. When you do stumble, you look at the whole picture of who you are rather than the blunders you make.

The farther along you travel on your spiritual path, the less you will need perfection within yourself or anyone else. So resist the urge to expect perfection in yourself and others; perfection is an illusion anyway! Instead, embrace your mistakes, for they deliver lessons that can help you to align with your spirit. Realizing this allows you to honor the light within you and everybody you meet. That is honoring your spirit and everyone else, too.

Keep this in mind as you continue along your journey: the more you learn, the more you will realize you don't have it all figured out--but the less you will feel a need to. You just have faith that each moment is meant to be. You'll come to realize that every episode of your life is part of what is intended for you. When you stumble and take notice, you will know there is a lesson that you are ready to learn—even if you don't recognize what it is in that moment. Everything in your life fits together like a puzzle. No, you won't always have all the pieces at once. Instead, you gather them along your journey. You come to accept that things are done in the right time and not on your time schedule—even your lessons. Best of all, you are comfortable with all of it.

Knowing that the lessons you receive will come in the right moment will also provide you with the comfort to slow down if necessary. When you feel that your soul has been hurt, it is important to give it the nourishment it needs. Often we pay attention to an ache in our bodies, but continue to push onward and neglect our soul when it has been harmed. When things happen that cause you to feel disconnected from spirit—either through your own actions or through no fault of your own—pause and bring yourself back to balance. Sometimes events in your life will cut you to the core, and sometimes you will feel drained of your will. Just as you would stop and get a bone set if it were broken, you need to stop and honor that your soul needs time to heal when it is affected.

Nourishing your soul means taking time to recuperate from life's hard blows and supporting your connection with spirit when you are status quo. You may experience loss, heartache, and other pain. You can get through anything, but it is important to acknowledge when something has an effect on you. When it does, allow yourself to heal by taking time off, meditating, getting away, or seeking professional help if needed. Allow your soul to reset itself in whatever way is effective for you. Doing things to nourish your soul on a regular basis, even when it is not weakened, will help to strengthen your connection with spirit and allow you to come back to balance more quickly. It will also lessen the severity of those unpleasant events when they do happen in your life.

Every person I have met, every job I have held, and every event in my life have made me the person

I am meant to be at this moment. If I had changed one single thing, I would not be the person I am today. If I hadn't felt pain, perhaps I wouldn't have the aptitude to understand what my clients are feeling. If I hadn't overcome obstacles, perhaps I wouldn't be able to motivate clients to overcome their own hurdles. If I hadn't experienced joy, unconditional love, loss, and triumph, I wouldn't be able to relate to others as well as I do. Most of all, if I hadn't felt all of these things, perhaps I wouldn't have been guided to nourish my soul and its connection to spirit, and to more fully comprehend the divine that exists within all of us. For that I am eternally grateful. Nourishing my soul has awarded me comfort through life's ups and downs, and it has heightened every triumph I have felt. You'll experience highs and lows. The key is to not keep yourself at the lows too long. You could miss something amazing. Strive for balance. When you are able to be kind to your spirit through any storm you are navigating, you are more equipped to have the courage to get the intended message, keep your peace, and be open to receiving the joys of everyday life.

19~With Faith, All Things Are Possible

It doesn't matter what your religious beliefs are; it *does* matter that you believe in something positive outside of yourself. It is not enough to say that you think there is something else out there but you don't know what. You are shortchanging yourself. Find out what. Not having a clear answer in regard to choosing a belief system is one of the few uncertainties that people are okay with. Until you know in your heart what you truly believe, you will not experience true unwavering faith. How could you? It just can't happen because you aren't sure what you have faith in.

If you want to have faith in good times and in bad, it is essential that you keep digging. Forget about what others say about religions and which ones are for you. Religions have stood the test of time because there is some "truth" to them. Nearly every organized religion has some similarities to one another. The differences, as far as I am concerned, are just humankind's misunderstandings in interpreting the word of God or their Creator. Let's keep in mind that all written word regarding religion was written by people. If you believe everything that your chosen religion is based on, that is your guidance. If you look at your religion more as having anecdotes with lessons from which you can learn to live your life, that is your choice, too. Ask yourself what sounds true to you. Ask yourself what *feels* right to you. Visit various houses of worship and ask yourself where you truly feel at home.

To begin understanding who or what you feel connected to, focus on your heart chakra, or the center of your chest, where your soul resides.

1) Close your eyes and begin to meditate.

2) As you meditate, allow yourself to be ushered to the part of you that is your direct connection to your Creator, your soul.

3) This is located in the center of your chest. It is the part of you without flaws. It is the part of you that asks if there is more to life. It is the part of you that seeks its purpose. It is the part that allows you to love unconditionally. It is the part that has true pride when you do something kind for someone. It is the "twinkle in your eyes." It is also the part of you that allows you to see yourself completely without judgment, as God or your Creator does.

4) Once you connect to that part of you, imagine a beautiful white light bridging your heart to that of your Creator.

5) When you reach the connection, you may feel an overwhelming feeling of unconditional love. You may feel complete peace or safety. It may feel like a comforting feeling that you have never known if you have never truly connected before.

6) Once you have that connection, ask:

    • Who are you? What should I call you?

    • What can I do to help strengthen my connection to you?

    • What can I do to better nourish my body?

    • What can I do to better nourish my mind?

    • What can I do to better nourish my soul?

7) Just listen, feel, and be open to whatever positive guidance you receive.

True faith comes from having a personal relationship with whoever you believe your Creator to be. It comes from feeling and experiencing the connection. With faith, all things really are possible. We have all heard age-old stories of individuals persevering against all odds with nothing but their faith, yet being able to triumph in the end. Maybe you have wished you had such faith but you just have a hard time believing. If you look at all of the religions in the world, you will see this story line repeated.

The Law of Attraction says we need to have a positive mindset. An integral part of working with the Law of Attraction is that you need to believe that it is possible for you to manifest your desires. What is this belief but another way of explaining faith? The Bible explains the importance of faith in God. Whatever it is that you believe in that is outside of yourself— be it God, a Creator, the universe, or some other positive symbol of a Higher Power— have faith that it/they/He/She has your back.

In honor of my fortieth birthday, I entered a triathlon and trained for months. The week before the event, I came down with a stomach virus. The night before the race I had such bad stomach cramps that I didn't sleep at all. The next morning, I attempted to eat something to settle my stomach and gain some strength. Nothing stayed down! The triathlon started at a park about an hour from my home, and I knew I was in no condition to drive. Thank goodness my husband drove me there.

I arrived at the site, stood at the starting line, and said, "If I am meant to complete this event, I will do it." At that moment I placed the outcome in God's hands. The starting gun sounded, and before I knew it, I had finished the swim phase. Then I got to the bike corral, changed into my biking gear, and prepared for the next phase.

Out on the bike loop I prayed, a lot. By the end of the biking portion, I felt reenergized. When I placed my bike in the corral to start the final phase of the three-part competition—the run—I knew I could finish.

No, I didn't finish in first place, but I did finish in the top half of all competitors. In my heart, I knew it wasn't me who completed that event. I felt

God's presence with me the whole time, giving me strength and courage to do what my body wasn't capable of doing that day.

Months later, I started training for a marathon. I had to slow my pace down and felt disappointed with my lack of progress. I've worked out since middle school. With all of my spiritual and physical training, I had thought I knew my body, but I had been overtraining. I was frustrated that I had become so out of touch, and I prayed for connection.

One beautiful hot summer day, I resumed my training. I didn't run fast but went at a pace that felt good. I was just glad to be back to my training. Not only could I continue toward my goal, but I also enjoyed that amazing feeling of connecting with my body. While jogging that day, I realized the prayer I'd made was answered.

Even more insight came to me as I climbed my second hill. Thinking that *with faith, all things are possible,* I was reminded of the triathlon I completed. As the warm breeze gently cooled my face and the sun beat down on my body, I noticed neighbors smiling and waving, people walking with their dogs, and horses neighing in the pastures. My whole neighborhood became even more beautiful than ever before! I realized this message, *with faith, all things are possible,* was relevant not only to my physical training-- but also to life and to everyone who desires deep connection. I saw the hills as life's obstacles and the endurance I was building as my faith that would endure whatever comes to me.

When the time came for me to run the marathon, I had already completed two 22-mile practice runs. My body was prepared, but I learned that life gives you choices and sometimes the insight you receive is about something different from what you think it is.

The weekend I was supposed to compete, my beloved golden retriever took a terrible turn for the worse with terminal cancer. I could not leave him. My family often joked that I loved Sam more than some people love their own children. He was born on my birthday and was the breed I had always wanted. Much to his credit, he was my motivation to fly across the country and learn Animal Reiki.

I was heartbroken and did not know what I was going to do without him. In my deepest despair, after he had passed, I once again was reminded of the message I received the day I was running: *With faith, all things are possible.* The message I learned that day wasn't just about whether I could or would do that race. It was a message that I found resonated very deeply within my soul as I wondered how I would overcome such a loss. Clearly, I was prepared physically to run, but my love for Sam made me choose him over any medal I would get for running a marathon. In my moment of sorrow, I found the message took on a different meaning depending on what I was facing in life. The message I received is one I am reminded of during any of life's obstacles when I feel like I am alone or have had all that I can handle. Although in one situation it served as re-assurance that God would be my physical strength when I felt weak, in this instance it reminded me that He would be my emotional strength to help me through a difficult loss. I knew that everything would be fine, and it was. I will take that message with me for my lifetime, and I invite you to do the same.

My faith has always been my support. It has seen me through life's obstacles for as long as I can remember. In my family, I had a strong example of what faith looked like in my grandfather, Poppie. As I recall, on one occasion he watched my brothers and me while my parents and grandmother visited my uncle in the hospital. At ages ten, eleven, and sixteen, we weren't an easy group to watch. I remember seeing Poppie sit quietly reading the Bible when suddenly he got a phone call. He had to go to the hospital because my uncle, his eldest son and namesake, wasn't going to make it through the night. Without hesitation, he loaded the three of us into his car to drive to the hospital. My parents and grandmother were already there, and they would all have to take turns to say their good-byes. Poppie was quiet, as he often was, on the drive, but even in this situation he never lost his patience with us. After my uncle had passed, when Poppie was grieving, he went to church. His faith helped him endure what no parent should have to experience: the loss of their child.

As a child, I heard another story about my grandfather and his personal relationship with God. He was the supervisor of the local creamery, which was an important job in our area at the time. On one occasion, there was a strike going on at the creamery. The supervisor was required to live in the home adjacent to the creamery, so he lived right next door to the striking employees. The minister of the very church that my grandfather and his whole family attended got upset with something involving the strike and shot at Poppie's home. Despite the minister clearly doing wrong, my grandfather continued to attend his church and worship, stating, "I am not there to worship the minister; I am there to worship God." That was such an important message for me, letting me know how important it is to not let a human's actions ever interfere with my relationship with God. We are all flawed as humans, even those in positions of religious power--some more than others. When we give others permission to be human and recognize them as such, we are able to keep our relationship with our Creator unaffected by whatever another person's actions are.

Poppie's faith was an integral part of his life. He didn't just say it; he lived it. I learned much more about faith through his actions than anything he ever said. He didn't celebrate his faith only on Sundays; he showed it daily in the way he treated others. I never heard him speak an unkind word about anyone. He was always the first to help people, and he kept his faith even in the toughest of times. Also, one of the characteristics that made him so profoundly genuine in his faith was that he never used it as an excuse to cast judgment on others. Now that I am an adult, I know that I was blessed to have him as a living testament of what a life of faith is. If you haven't seen faith of this strength in your own life, allow these stories and the stories of others you know to motivate you to find your own faith.

It is easy to have a strong faith when things are good. A strong faith also weathers the storms of life and is there regardless of what you are experiencing. In my experience, the more open you are to experiencing faith, the more easily you can call on it in times of need. Just like with any of the other suggestions in this book, you will find that with practice, experiencing faith will become easier, it will come more naturally, and you will develop strength you can call upon under any circumstance.

Ten Ways to Maintain a Balanced Life

1) It's okay to say no. In fact, sometimes it's a great thing!

2) Do something you enjoy every day—even if only for five minutes.

3) You can't please everybody, so please yourself first. (Remember, if it is dedicated to your highest good, it is dedicated to everybody's highest good!)

4) Schedule "you" time on your calendar just like other important appointments.

5) Set your priorities for the day and stick to them.

6) Don't allow others to interrupt your schedule with their issues.

7) Limit time spent on social media and phone calls that aren't related to the priorities you've set for the day.

8) Recharge. Spend time in nature. Meditate, exercise, and nourish your body, mind, and spirit.

9) Ask for help whenever you need it.

10) Live in the moment. Be open to good things coming your way. Remember, *with faith, all things are possible!*

Every day is a gift. When you expect a great life, you'll have one. You get to choose at every moment how you will spend your precious time. If you start to look at your time as something valuable, the same way some people look at currency, you may be more willing to balance it and "spend" it doing things that are important to you. Make the shift in your perspective with whatever is meaningful to you.

20~Crashing the Wave of Complacency

Have you ever heard the phrase *a little knowledge is dangerous*? It applies to people who become too comfortable with the knowledge they have. When we first begin studying a subject, it can be overwhelming. After hard work we can get to a place that feels comfortable to us, even though it may be relatively early in our studies. This should be viewed as more of a "plateau" than an ending. If your complacency is left unchecked, you could ride the wave of what you know now and stop searching. But eventually that wave crashes.

Does this apply to you? If you're in denial about what you need in order to heal, you may experience these triggers:

1) You believe you can fix everyone around you.

2) You think you can heal yourself by helping others.

3) You see nothing in yourself that may be a developmental issue.

4) You feel the need to judge others and compare your spiritual progress to theirs.

5) You believe others don't *get* you because you are more advanced than they are.

6) You constantly feel sorry for strangers you meet in passing. You think it is your job to fix them even when they haven't asked for your help.

7) You have uncontrollable urges to give advice to everybody you meet.

8) You believe you are "done" healing. You have healed your body-mind-spirit of all effects of living your life thus far. You have *no* baggage.

9) You think you've already mastered all the material in every spiritual book written and have nothing left to learn.

10) You can't acknowledge that what you dislike in others is actually what you dislike in yourself.

11) You no longer get along with anyone around you because you *think* you are too spiritual and they have not grown.

If you trust in the process and enjoy the journey, you will realize that you are meant to learn throughout your whole life. Spiritual studies should not be viewed as a sprint. They should be viewed as a marathon. When you slow down and just enjoy the process, you can enjoy every step in your development. It takes thought, motivation, and faith to push through your beliefs and continue your journey toward self-actualization. Don't delay addressing them!

A 21-Day Challenge that Can Change Your Life

Let's combine many of the tools that you have acquired while reading this book into a challenge that can change your life. Many believe it takes 21 days to make or break a habit. All of these tools are new habits to help you to manifest your desires and maintain peace. I am challenging you to stick with the following program for just 21 days. Once that period is over, if you would like to go back to your old ways, that is your choice to make. If you follow this plan for the full 21 days, by the time it is over you may have instilled this plan as habit. You may also see so many positive changes in your life that you won't want to give the plan up! So I challenge you: give it 21 days—but-- be careful because this plan may be habit-forming.

Put all the information you've been reading into practice:

- Meditate or unwind for at least five minutes a day—quiet time just for you.

- Schedule something you enjoy every day.

- To prepare for the morning, do something special for yourself the night before.

- Exercise if you are healthy enough to do so.

- Eat a well-balanced diet.

- Be authentic.

- Tune in to your intuition.

- Follow "Ten Ways to Maintain a Balanced Life"

- Sign the "Contract with Yourself to Be Positive."

- On the calendar that follows, document all of the positive things you experience each day. Be grateful for each positive experience, big or small.

- Reflect on where you think your desires are coming from. Who/What do you feel a connection with? Give thanks to your Creator!

Stick to this practice for 21 days. Agree to celebrate the positives, both big and small. Focus on your desires, and remain grateful for everything. At the end of 21 days, you'll find you have not only changed your thinking, but you have begun to change your life. What will you create in your life? Can you devote less than an hour a day to finding peace and maintaining it regardless of what happens around you?

Take 21 days to devote to your desires. On the calendar that follows, fill in everything you are thankful for each day. Record everything, not just the big stuff. As you stay focused on the exercise, you will begin to create the habit of looking for what you are grateful for. As you acknowledge this, you will create a domino effect of more positivity and greater abundance in your life.

Example: Document what you are grateful for day by day for 21 days.

DAY 1	DAY 2	DAY 3	DAY 4	DAY 5	DAY 6	DAY 7
Lunch w/ friends	Free half-day at work; free time to finish my project	A special gift for no reason	A call from a close friend	Some-body let me cut in in busy traffic.	A remod-eled living room. It feels great!	A smile for no reason

DAY 8	DAY 9	DAY 10	DAY 11	DAY 12	DAY 13	DAY 14
Feeling extra strong dur-ing my workout	Surprise from my hubby	A hug from my friend	A nice sunny day	Free coffee	A call from my mom	Fun with friends

DAY 15	DAY 16	DAY 17	DAY 18	DAY 19	DAY 20	DAY 21
A new grateful client	A call from an old friend	A thank you e-mail	A visit from family	A sum of money that I did not expect to receive	Feeling extremely strong on my run today	A.M. "family time"

Document what you are grateful for day by day for 21 days.

DAY 1	DAY 2	DAY 3	DAY 4	DAY 5	DAY 6	DAY 7

DAY 8	DAY 9	DAY 10	DAY 11	DAY 12	DAY 13	DAY 14

DAY 15	DAY 16	DAY 17	DAY 18	DAY 19	DAY 20	DAY 21

Making a Contract with Yourself to Be Positive

The act of committing to something, whether it is through a legal contract or a less formal means like what is shown here, holds us more accountable to what is put in place. It is almost as if a switch goes on within our internal workings, causing the change to take effect from that moment. There is an inner desire within all of us that motivates us to stick to agreements that we put in place. I encourage you to make a copy of this agreement, sign it, and post it where you can see it daily. Hold yourself accountable for the changes that you intend to put into effect. The possibilities are endless!

Moving forward, I agree to be positive as often as I possibly can. I understand that the more positive I am, the more positivity I bring into my life. In the event that something doesn't turn out the way I expect, I will be open to believing that something better is on the horizon. I will give thanks every day for each blessing, big or small, for I know I am blessed.

From this moment on, I agree to catch myself when I attempt to give power to the things I don't like in my life. I release myself from jealousy, gossip, and complaining. They don't serve me, but rather waste my time and bring me more negativity. I choose peace, love, and joy.

PRINT NAME: _____

SIGNED: _____

DATE:_____

Ten Things to Remember During Your 21-Day Challenge

The 21-day challenge is a process to instill in your life the new habits you desire. The challenge may feel awkward at first. You may feel "wobbly" like you did when you were a child learning to ride your bike without training wheels. As you continue to practice, however, you will notice before long that it becomes second nature. You will be instilling new positive tools deep within that will be available to you whenever you wish to use them. Once you have mastered these tools, it will indeed be second nature—like riding a bike.

1) This is for you. If others don't understand or share in your excitement, that is okay. This challenge was created to blend the tools you have learned into your lifestyle so you can begin to experience the changes that you desire in your life and find peace.

2) When you have setbacks, focus on the moment and turn the situation around.

3) Avoid negative people who don't want you to change. Misery loves company.

4) Remember, in the long run it takes less effort to be upbeat.

5) Nobody can do this challenge for you, but you can ask for help along the way. Choose your "helpers" wisely.

6) It's about seeing the perfection in imperfection, not misleading yourself into thinking life will be perfect.

7) If you find you aren't changing those areas where you desire change, question what's beneficial about staying where you are.

8) Find the positive even in the negatives.

9) Look for the beauty in the world, and more will come to you.

10) Bring your thoughts back to the good in your life. That will bring you peace.

21~Keep Going Until You Collect Your Prize

It's only natural to be excited about what you feel, see, or sense your life is becoming. You may be tempted to tell the good news to everyone you know. If you share your new perspective on life with others, be cautious of friends or family members who try to pull you back to where you were. Along your journey, people will challenge you. Reassuring both you and themselves in the face of their own insecurities, they will try to shift you to their belief system. When you begin to move forward, it can be threatening to some of those around you who may choose not to do so. Often they attempt to change your mind to "protect you" or to help you be "reasonable." Some people may actually believe they *are* protecting you.

Keep in mind that just because you've changed that doesn't mean the people in your life have changed. Others remain unaffected by the transformation you've gone through. They only know that *you* have changed, and that feels uncomfortable for them. They may offer "proof" that this shift doesn't work, but that "proof" belongs to them to support their "truth." Don't make it yours. If you accept their proof, it's an easy slide back to your former life—after all you've accomplished. It's just as easy to provide "proof" that it *does* work. Hold onto that from now on! Stand in your power. You established early on that your old way of thinking hasn't worked for you, or you wouldn't still be reading this book.

As you continue this new way of thinking, accept that some people may leave your life, while others may begin to change with you. I encourage you to stay strong. You don't have to get into a belief war with everyone who doesn't share your views. Choose whom you will discuss your views with and whom you will not. Some individuals won't agree with your way of thinking, and some will. Let's face it, not everyone agrees on everything, and that's okay. This journey is not about them; it's something you're doing for yourself. Your life will be whatever *you* intend it to be— no one else. Visualize, feel, taste, hear, and manifest. Anything less is stopping short of what was meant for you. Step into your greatness. Don't fear it or doubt it. It's meant for you. Know this: when your life starts to flow beautifully, people may become curious about the new mystery you hold. Yet it's not a mystery at all; it's life as it is meant to be lived.

Don't get me wrong. I'm not saying to never take anyone's helpful ideas unless they are your own. Keep in mind that divine guidance can come to you *through others*. They can tell you exactly what you need to know at pivotal times in your life. I'm saying do not discount what you absolutely *know* is right for you just because others don't agree with your plans. There's a big difference between taking what's helpful and allowing somebody's negative thinking to take you on a distracting detour.

Know that if you're doing the right thing *for* you, it should feel right *to* you. The unrest, fears, and worries that go with pondering issues for days, weeks, months, and even years happen when you force yourself into being comfortable with something that deep down isn't right for you.

What is *your* purpose for being here? Whether you're still laying the groundwork or ready to walk through the door, your intuition encourages you to get going. Ask, "What am I meant to do in this world? What will be my legacy?"

Never discount the impact that you as one person will have on any one individual or organization. Perhaps merely being in a particular location will help you to live out your legacy in one way or another.

Life isn't about existing, but experiencing each moment through your soul. You are a beautiful child of your Creator with a purpose and unique skills to help you fulfill it. Be who you are meant to be. Hold onto your power. You are the person in charge of your journey. Let the words of naysayers fall on deaf ears. Stay focused on the prize at the end. Peace will be yours for being true to yourself, and to what you know is meant to be your legacy.

I wish you peace, love, and joy beyond your greatest imagination!

Wrap-Up—Twelve Ways of Being

As a reminder, here's a list of 12 ways of "being," for enjoying a peaceful mind amid chaos in our out-of-control world:

1) Caring for your body

2) Eating healthily

3) Exercising

4) Connecting with your spirit and your source/Creator

5) Trusting your own ability to make the right decision for your highest good

6) Looking for the positive, not the negative

7) Knowing there's a reason for everything

8) Being fully grateful

9) Being your authentic self

10) Cherishing the good moments in your life

11) Looking for the lessons in your experiences and moving on

12) Focusing on your goal, not stopping short of claiming the prize: the life you desire

You are exactly where you are meant to be. Losing sight of that will only distract you from all of the good that's in your life. Use what you've learned to *stop* going through the motions of life, and *start* living it your way. You'll be amazed at the journey that unfolds.

A BIT ABOUT THE AUTHOR...

Cindy Nolte is a television talk show host, keynote speaker, and she runs a private practice in which she offers workshops, certifications, hypnosis, past-life regression, and energy work. She is a certified hypnotist, hypnosis instructor, energy practitioner, teacher, mentor, intuitive, group fitness instructor, and consultant. Cindy takes the mind-body-spirit connection very seriously, acknowledging that they all must be nourished to create optimum health and wellness. Cindy is the founder of Fresh Look on Life, where with great honor, she assists her clients in uncovering the answers that they hold within. For more information on Cindy Nolte, her practice, workshops, or her television show, check out **www. freshlookonlife.com**.

Made in the USA
Charleston, SC
25 July 2015